D1538327

▶Select Readings

Intermediate

Linda Lee
Erik Gunder

OXFORD
UNIVERSITY PRESS

OXFORD
UNIVERSITY PRESS

198 Madison Avenue, New York, NY 10016 USA
Great Clarendon Street, Oxford OX2 6DP England

Oxford University Press is a department of the University of Oxford. It furthers the University's objective of excellence in research, scholarship, and education by publishing worldwide in

Oxford New York
Auckland Bangkok Buenos Aires Cape Town
Chennai Dar es Salaam Delhi Hong Kong
Istanbul Karachi Kolkata Kuala Lumpur
Madrid Melbourne Mexico City Mumbai
Nairobi São Paulo Shanghai
Taipei Tokyo Toronto

OXFORD is a registered trademark of Oxford University Press.

ISBN 0–19–437475–0

Published in the United States by Oxford University Press, New York

Copyright © 2001 Oxford University Press

Library of Congress Cataloging-in-Publication Data

Lee, Linda, 1950–
    Select readings intermediate / by Linda Lee and Erik Gundersen.
        p.cm.
    ISBN 0–19–437475–0
    1. English language-Textbooks for foreign speakers.
    2. Readers. I. Gundersen, Erik. II. Title.

PE1128.L426 2000
428.6´4-dc21   00–029125

Editorial Manager: Chris Foley
Developmental Editor: Chris Balderston
Project Editor: Mary C. D'Apice
Production Editor: Maura Tukey
Contributing Editor: Paul MacIntyre
Photo Researcher: Maura Tukey
Designer: Susan Brorein
Cover Design: Tom Hawley, Hawley Design
Production Controller: Shanta Persaud
Production and Prepress Services: Compset, Inc.

Printing (last digit): 10

Printed in Hong Kong.

ACKNOWLEDGMENTS

Illustration by: Glenn Harrington

The publishers would like to thank the following for their permission to reproduce photographs: CNP/Archive Photos, Frank Capri/SAGA/Archive Photos, Boston Globe, ©Bettmann/CORBIS, Mike Brinson/The Image Bank 1999, Sung Chihhsiung, Ghislain and Marie David de Lossy/The Image Bank 1999, China Tourism Press/ Yang Liu/The Image Bank 1999, ©1993 Bill McDowell, Christie's Images/SuperStock, Tom Rosenthal/ SuperStock, Frank Siteman/©Tony Stone Images.

The publishers would also like to thank the following for their permission to reproduce text excerpts:

"A Long Walk Home" provided courtesy of the author, Jason Bocarro

"Getting Ready for the Message" from *Your College Experience, Expanded Reader Edition, 3rd Edition*, by J.N. Gardner and A.J. Jewler ©1997. Reprinted with permission of Wadsworth, a division of Thomson Learning. Fax 800 730–2215

"Culture Shock" courtesy of the author, Bob Weinstein.

"A Young Blind Whiz on Computers Makes a Name in Industry" provided courtesy of *The Wall Street Journal* and the Copyright Clearance Center.

"Pop Group Enigma's Use of Taiwan Folk Song Stirs Debate" © copyright NPR® 1999. The news report by NPR's Frank Koller was originally broadcast on NPR's "All Things Considered®" on June 11, 1999, and is used with the permission of National Public Radio, Inc. Any unauthorized duplication is strictly prohibited.

"The Enigma Archives" courtesy of Gavin Stok

"How to Make a Speech" by George Plimpton, from *How to Use the Power of the Printed Word* edited by Billings S. Fuess, copyright © 1985 by International Paper Company. Used by permission of Doubleday, a division of Random House, Inc.

"Private Lives" courtesy of the author, Diane Daniel. Interview with Bill Gates, pp.78–85 from *Future Talk* by Larry King. Copyright 1998 by Larry King. Reprinted by permission of HarperCollins Publishers, Inc.

"Letters of Application" from *Business Letters the Easy Way* by Andrea B. Geffner.

"Before, During and After a Job Interview" provided courtesy of the author, Peggy Schmidt.

"Out to Lunch" provided courtesy of Joe Robinson and ESCAPE Magazine, www.escapemag.com

"Public Attitudes Toward Science" from *Black Holes and Baby Universes and Other Essays* by Stephen W. Hawking. Copyright © 1993 by Stephen W. Hawking. Used by permission of Bantam Books, a division of Random House, Inc.

"John's Taiwanese Wedding" provided courtesy of the authors John Felty and Bill McDowell.

"Thinking Like a Genius" originally appeared in May 1998 issue of *The Futurist*. Used with permission from the World Future Society, 7910 Woodmont Avenue, Suite 450, Bethesda, Maryland 20814. 301/656–8274. http://www.wfs.org

"Conversational Ball Games" provided courtesy of the author, Nancy Sakamoto.

▶ Acknowledgments

The publisher would like to thank the following teachers whose comments, reviews and assistance were instrumental in the development of *Select Readings*:

Ann Mei-Yu Chang
Ann-Marie Hadzima
Beatrice Hsiao-Tsui Yang
Brett Reynolds
Chia-Yi Sun
Chi-Fan Lin
Ching-Kang Liu
Christine Chen-Ju Chen
Chuan-Ta Chao
Colin Gullberg
David W.Y. Dai
Douglas I-Ping Ho
Florence Yi-Hui Chiou
Fujiko Sano
Hsiu-Chieh Chen
Hyung-Gu Lee
Jessica Hsin-Hwa Chen
Jong-Bok Kim
Joyce Yu-Hua Lee
Kabyong Park
Kun-liang Chuang

Lee Hyun Woo
Maggie Sokolik
Maureen Chiu-Yu Tseng
Meredith Pike-Baky
Maosung Lin
Monica Li-Feng Kuo
Patricia Pei-Chun Che
Paul Cameron
Pei-Yin Lu
Peng-Hsiang Chen
Richard Solomons
Robin Cheng-Hsing Tsai
Sherry Hsin-Ying Li
Stella Wen-Hui Li
Susan Shu-Hua Chou
Tsuh-Lai Huang
Won Park
Ying-Chien Chang
Yu-Chen Hsu
Yun Jong Ryol

The authors would like to thank the following OUP staff for their support and assistance in the development of *Select Readings*:

Julia Chang
Tina Chen
Coco Cheng
Ted Yoshioka
JJ Lee
Chang Oh Lim

Hyun Jeong Lee
Hyun Joo Kim
Paul Riley
Sumio Takiguchi
Toshiki Matsuda
Alison Kane

Aya Ikeuchi
Ally McPhee
Ken Kamoshita
Tim Cupp
Mari Muramatsu

Special thanks to Chris Foley, Chris Balderston, Mary D'Apice, Paul MacIntyre, and Maura Tukey for all of your insights, guidance, and suggestions for change throughout the editorial process. Working with you has been a great pleasure.

Heartfelt thanks to Peter, Jimmy, and Diane for all of your encouragement, support, and love—Erik Gundersen.

▶ Contents

► Scope and Sequence

	Content	Reading Skill	Building Vocabulary	Language Focus
Chapter 1 A Long Walk Home	Father teaches son a lesson	Using context	Phrasal verbs	Past Perfect
Chapter 2 Student Learning Teams	How to work in groups with classmates	Skimming	Team-related words and phrases	Subject gerunds
Chapter 3 Culture Shock	An exchange student in the U.S.	Topic vs. Main idea	Learning new expressions	*used to, get used to, be used to*
Chapter 4 A Young Blind Whiz	Disability leads to success	Inferencing	Compound nouns	Reduced clauses
Chapter 5 Pop Group's Use of Folk Song Stirs Debate	Who owns the rights to folk music?	Scanning	Grouping words	Present perfect
Chapter 6 How to Make a Speech	The art of good speech making	Using headings	Powerful verbs	Imperatives
Chapter 7 Private Lives	A special place for reflection	Supporting main ideas	Using context to guess meaning	Talking about the past

▶ Scope and Sequence

	Content	Reading Skill	Building Vocabulary	Language Focus
Chapter 8 Future Talk	An interview with Bill Gates about the future	Using context	Word forms	*too/enough*
Chapter 9 Letters of Application	Applying for jobs effectively in writing	Reading instructional materials	Using connecting words	Giving advice
Chapter 10 Out to Lunch	Spanish siesta tradition	Finding details	Word forms	*It's* + adj. +inf.
Chapter 11 Public Attitudes Toward Science	How can the public be helped to understand science?	Main ideas	Keeping a vocabulary notebook	Using passive voice
Chapter 12 John's Taiwanese Wedding	Humorous misunder-standing in an intercultural wedding	Inferencing	Synonyms (adjectives and adverbs)	Subjunctive verbs
Chapter 13 The Art of Genius	Ways that geniuses think	Using examples	Grouping words	Understand-ing the use of colons
Chapter 14 Conversational Ball Games	English and Japanese conversations	Patterns of organization	Prefixes	Conditional statements

► Introduction

To the Teacher

Select Readings is a reading text for intermediate students of English. In ***Select Readings,*** high-interest, authentic reading passages serve as springboards for reading skills development, vocabulary building, language analysis, and thought-provoking discussions and writing.

The readings represent a wide range of genres (newspaper and magazine articles, personal essays, textbook chapters, book excerpts, on-line discussions, and interviews) gathered from well-respected sources such as *The Wall Street Journal,* the *Utne Reader,* and *National Public Radio.*

General Approach to Reading Instruction

The following principles have guided our approach throughout the development of ***Select Readings:***

- **Exposing students to a variety of text types and genres helps them develop more effective reading skills.** Students learn to handle the richness and depth of writing styles they will encounter as they read more widely in English.

- **Readers become engaged with a selection when they are asked to respond personally to its theme.** While comprehension questions help students see if they have understood the information in a reading, discussion questions ask students to consider the issues raised by the passage.

- **Readers sharpen their reading, vocabulary-building, and language analysis skills when skills work is tied directly to the content and language of each reading passage.** This book introduces students to reading skills such as skimming and scanning, vocabulary-building strategies such as finding synonyms and using phrasal verbs, and language study topics such as reduced clauses.

- **Good readers make good writers.** Reading helps students develop writing skills, while writing experience helps students become better readers.

- **Background knowledge plays an important role in reading comprehension.** An important goal of *Select Readings* is to illustrate how thinking in advance about the topic of a reading prepares readers to better comprehend and interact with a text.

Chapter Overview

Each chapter in *Select Readings* includes the eight sections described below. Suggested time frames for covering the material are also given.

1. Opening Page (5 to 15 minutes)

The purpose of this page is to draw readers into the theme and content of the chapter.

Teaching Suggestions:

- Call students' attention to the chapter focus box. Give them a chance to think about the content and skills they are about to study and to set their own learning goals for the chapter.

- Ask students to identify what they see in the photo(s) or artwork on the page and guess what the chapter is about. Have them read the quotation, restate it in their own words, and then say if they agree with it. Finally, ask what connection there might be between the images and the quotation.

2. Before You Read (30 to 40 minutes)

One question in each *Before You Read* section asks students to reflect on their prior knowledge of the chapter's topic. Giving students time to think about and discuss this question is an essential part of helping them activate their background knowledge on the topic. A second activity in the *Before You Read* section invites students to practice pre-reading skills such as skimming and scanning. Effective readers use these pre-reading skills regularly to get an initial feel for the content and organization of the reading passage.

Teaching Suggestions:

- Make sure that students understand the purpose of the *Before You Read* activities. Explain that activating prior knowledge will help them to better comprehend the reading passage.

- Encourage student participation in the activities by having people work in small groups to complete the activities.

- React to the content of students' ideas rather than to the grammatical accuracy of their responses.

3. Reading Passage (45 to 60 minutes)

In general, the readings become increasingly long and more complex as the chapters progress. To help students successfully tackle each passage we have provided the following support tools:

Vocabulary glosses. Challenging words and expressions are glossed throughout the readings. In most cases, we have glossed chunks of words (e.g., *shirk his responsibility*) instead of individual vocabulary items (e.g., *shirk*). This approach helps students develop a better sense of how important context is to understanding the meaning of new words.

Culture and Language Notes. On pages 168–189, students will find explanations for cultural references and language usage that appear in blue type in the readings. Notes are provided on a wide range of topics from scientific information such as acid rain, to geographical references such as Madrid, to famous people such as Mark Twain.

Numbered lines. For easy reference every fifth line of each reading passage is numbered.

Recorded reading passages. Listening to someone reading a text aloud helps language learners see how words are grouped in meaningful chunks, thus aiding comprehension.

At the end of each reading, there is a short section giving biographical information on the author or information about the source. This information helps students develop a richer context for the perspective of each author.

Teaching Suggestions:

- Encourage students to read actively. Circling words, writing questions in the margins, and taking notes are three ways in which students can make reading a more active and meaningful experience.

- Make sure students know how to use the vocabulary glosses, *Culture Notes*, and other support tools to assist them in the reading process.

- Encourage students to use context to guess the meaning of unfamiliar words.

- Play the recorded version of the reading passage and ask students to listen to how the reader groups words together. As they listen to the recording, students can lightly underline or circle the groups of words.

4. After You Read: Understanding the Text (30 to 45 minutes)

Following each reading, there are two post-reading activities that give students the chance to (a) clarify their understanding of the text, and

(b) discuss the issues raised in the reading. The comprehension questions are for students to work through on their own. Questions in the *Consider the Issues* section, on the other hand, ask students to talk about ideas introduced in the reading.

Teaching Suggestions:

- Get students to discuss their reactions to the readings in pairs or groups. The process of discussing questions and answers gives students an opportunity to check their comprehension more critically and analyze their reactions to the passages.

- Show students the value of returning to the reading again and again to answer the comprehension and discussion questions. Ask them to point out the specific places in the reading where they have found answers to the questions posed.

- If time permits and you would like students to have additional writing practice, ask them to write an essay or a journal entry on one of the questions in the *Consider the Issues* section.

5. Reading Skills (20 to 30 minutes)

At the beginning of each *Reading Skills* section, students encounter a short explanation of the skill in focus and, when appropriate, an example of how that skill relates to the reading in the chapter. The task following this explanation asks students to return to the reading to think about and apply a new reading skill.

Teaching Suggestions:

- Discuss the general purpose of developing reading skills. The more students understand the rationale behind acquiring these critical skills, the more motivated they will be to develop and refine them.

- Review the explanations and sample sentences at the beginning of each *Reading Skills* section before asking students to tackle the questions that follow. Encourage them to ask any questions they have about the explanations or examples.

- Reflect with students on the ways in which they can apply the reading skills they have learned in each chapter to other reading passages and to other reading genres.

6. Building Vocabulary (20 to 30 minutes)

Reading extensively is an excellent way for students to increase their vocabulary base. Considering this, we pay careful attention to developing students' vocabulary-building skills in each chapter of

Select Readings. Understanding phrasal verbs, working with word forms, finding synonyms, and a variety of other vocabulary-building skills are taught throughout the book. Like the reading skill activities, each *Building Vocabulary* section starts out with a short explanation and, when appropriate, examples of the skill in focus. In the activity that follows the explanation, students typically scan the reading to gather and analyze various types of words.

Teaching Suggestions:

- Review the explanations and sample sentences at the beginning of each *Building Vocabulary* section before asking students to tackle the questions that follow. Encourage them to ask any questions they have about the explanations or examples.

- Show students the value of returning to the reading to find an answer whenever they are unsure of a vocabulary-related question.

- Encourage students to keep a vocabulary notebook. Present various ways in which students can organize the words in their notebook: by chapter, by topic, by part of speech, etc.

- Discuss the value of using an English-English learner's dictionary to find the meanings of unfamiliar words.

7. Language Focus (20 to 30 minutes)

The final skill-building section in each chapter calls attention to important grammatical structures and functions that occur with some degree of frequency in the reading passage. The goal of this section is to focus students' attention on critical grammar points as they occur in context.

Teaching Suggestions:

- Review the explanations and sample sentences at the beginning of each *Language Focus* section before asking students to tackle the questions that follow. Encourage students to ask any questions they have about the explanations or examples.

- Invite students to talk about what they already know about the language point in focus. Many students know a great deal about grammar and are pleased to demonstrate this knowledge.

- Underscore the fact that the *Language Focus* sections are intended to help students review language they have already learned in the context of an authentic reading passage. It can be very valuable for students to see the ways in which grammatical structures they have studied appear naturally in real-life reading selections.

8. Discussion and Writing (45 to 60 minutes)

At the end of each chapter, students have an opportunity to talk and write about a variety of issues. The questions in this section provide students with a chance to broaden their view on the topic of the reading and to address more global issues and concerns.

Teaching Suggestions:

- When time permits, let students discuss a question a second time with a different partner or group. This allows them to apply what they learned in their first discussion of the question.

- Choose one or more of the questions in this section as an essay topic for students.

Bonus Features

Crossword Puzzles. At the end of each chapter, you will find a crossword puzzle that recycles and reviews some of the key vocabulary from the reading. These puzzles can be used as homework, as optional activities for groups or individuals who finish other exercises early, or as review activities several weeks after completing a chapter.

Maps. Each location mentioned in a reading passage is clearly marked on one of the maps found on pages 190–193.

This project grew out of our deep and profound love for reading, and for sharing this love of reading with our students. In developing *Select Readings,* we have enjoyed the process of talking to teachers all over the world about the types of authentic selections they feel their students enjoy the most, and learn the most from. We hope that you and your students enjoy teaching and learning with *Select Readings.*

Linda Lee

Erik Gundersen

Chapter Focus

CONTENT:
Learning an important
lesson

READING SKILL:
Using context

*BUILDING
VOCABULARY:*
Phrasal verbs

LANGUAGE FOCUS:
Past perfect

*"Mistakes are a fact
of life. It is the
response to error
that counts."*

– *Nikki Giovanni*
American writer
(1943 –)

Chapter ▲ **1** A Long Walk Home

Before You Read

1. In the story on pages 4–5, a young man tells a lie. Do you think it's ever OK to tell a lie? If so, when?

2. Read the title of the story and predict what the story is about.

3. Read the first sentence in the first, second, and third paragraphs. Now what do you think the story is about? Share your ideas with a partner.

A LONG WALK HOME

by Jason Bocarro

from *Chicken Soup for the Teenage Soul*

Note: Explanations for words in blue type can be found in the Culture and Language Notes on pages 168–189

1   I grew up in the south of **Spain** in a little community called Estepona. I was 16 when one morning, my father told me I could drive him into a remote village called Mijas, about 18 miles away, on the condition that I take[1] the car in to be serviced[2] at a nearby garage. Having just
5   learned to drive and hardly ever having the opportunity to use the car, I readily accepted. I drove Dad into Mijas and promised to pick him up at 4 p.m., then drove to a nearby garage and dropped off the car. Because I had a few hours to spare,[3] I decided to catch a couple of movies at a theater near the garage. However, I became so immersed[4]
10   in the films that I completely lost track of time.[5] When the last movie had finished, I looked down at my watch. It was six o'clock. I was two hours late!

     I knew Dad would be angry if he found out I'd been watching movies. He'd never let me drive again. I decided to tell him that the
15   car needed some repairs and that they had taken longer than had been expected. I drove up to the place where we had planned to meet and saw Dad waiting patiently on the corner. I apologized for being late and told him that I'd come as quickly as I could, but the car had needed some major repairs. I'll never forget the look he gave me.[6]

20   "I'm disappointed that you feel you have to lie to me, Jason."

     "What do you mean? I'm telling the truth."

     Dad looked at me again. "When you did not show up, I called the garage to ask if there were any problems, and they told me that you had not yet picked up the car. So you see, I know there were no
25   problems with the car." A rush of guilt ran through me as I feebly confessed to[7] my trip to the movie theater and the real reason for my tardiness. Dad listened intently as a sadness passed through him.

---

[1] **on the condition that I take**   if I took

[2] **to be serviced**   to be checked for problems and repaired if necessary

[3] **had a few hours to spare**   had a few free hours

[4] **immersed**   interested in, fascinated by

[5] **lost track of time**   didn't pay attention to the time

[6] **the look he gave me**   the way he looked at me

[7] **confessed to**   told the truth about

"I'm angry, not with you but with myself. You see, I realize that I
have failed as a father if after all these years you feel that you have to
30   lie to me. I have failed because I have brought up a son who cannot
even tell the truth to his own father. I'm going to walk home now and
contemplate[8] where I have gone wrong all these years."

"But Dad, it's 18 **miles** to home. It's dark. You can't walk home."

My protests, my apologies and the rest of my utterances were
35   useless. I had let my father down,[9] and I was about to learn one of the
most painful lessons of my life. Dad began walking along the dusty
roads. I quickly jumped in the car and followed behind, hoping he
would relent.[10] I pleaded all the way, telling him how sorry I was, but
he simply ignored me, continuing on silently, thoughtfully and
40   painfully. For 18 miles I drove behind him, averaging about five miles
per hour.

Seeing my father in so much physical and emotional pain was the
most distressing and painful experience that I have ever faced.
However, it was also the most successful lesson. I have never lied to
45   him since.

About the Source

Chicken Soup for the Teenage Soul is just one of many
best-selling books in the *Chicken Soup for the Soul* series, edited by
Jack Canfield and Mark Victor Hansen. Chicken soup is traditionally
thought to be an extremely healthy food that can cure sickness and
give comfort. The title of these books suggests that reading the
stories within them can have a healthy affect on the soul or spirit.
The stories in the books are all taken from real life.

---

[8] **contemplate**   think seriously about
[9] **let my father down**   disappointed my father
[10] **relent**   do what he said he wouldn't do (i.e., ride home in the car)

After You Read

Understanding the Text

A. Events in the Story

1. **Order the events.** Number the events in the story "A Long Walk Home" from the first (1) to the last (10).

   _6_ He apologized to his father for being late.

   _3_ He went to a movie theater.

   _2_ He dropped the car off at a garage to be serviced.

   _8_ He realized his father knew he was lying.

   _5_ He realized it was six o'clock and his father was waiting for him.

   _10_ He followed his father the whole 18 miles home.

   _4_ He picked up the car at the garage and then went to pick up his father.

   _7_ He told his father a lie.

   _1_ Jason drove his father into town and dropped him off.

   _9_ He tried to persuade his father to get into the car.

2. In your own words, retell the story "A Long Walk Home."

B. Consider the issues. Work with a partner to answer the questions below.

1. What do you think Jason said when he apologized to his father for being late?

2. What is your opinion of the way Jason's father responded to his son's lie?

3. Jason said that he learned something from this experience. Besides learning not to lie, what do you think he learned?

Using context

When you read, you can use context (the surrounding words and ideas) to guess the meaning of many unfamiliar words.

A. In the sentences below, use context to guess the meaning of the italicized words. Circle the letter of your answer.

1. I was 16 when one morning, my father told me I could drive him into a remote village called Mijas, about 18 miles away, on the condition that I take the car in to be serviced at a nearby *garage*.

   a. building **b.** restaurant **c.** repair shop

2. Having just learned to drive, and hardly ever having the opportunity to use the car, I *readily* accepted.

   a. quickly **b.** quietly **c.** sadly

3. Because I had a few hours to spare, I decided to *catch* a couple of movies at a theater near the garage.

   a. find **b.** watch **c.** ignore

4. My protests, my apologies, and the rest of my *utterances* were useless.

   a. friends **b.** clothes **c.** words

B. See how much information you can get from context. Use the words and ideas in the rest of the sentence to guess the missing word(s). There are many possible answers.

1. When I _____got_____ to the garage to pick up the car, they said it wasn't ready yet.

2. I went to a nearby ____theater____ to watch a couple of movies.

3. When I ____looked____ at my watch, I saw that it was already six o'clock.

4. I _____got_____ the movie theater as soon as the movie had finished.

Phrasal verbs

Phrasal verbs have two or three parts: a verb and one or two other words like *down, up, off,* or *out.* Many phrasal verbs are difficult to understand because the two or three words together have a special meaning.

*I **grew up** in the south of Spain.*
*I **let** my father **down** when I lied to him.*

A. Underline the phrasal verbs in the sentences below. Then use context to guess the meaning of each verb. Share your answers with a partner.

1. When Jason's father <u>found out</u> that his son had been watching movies, he was very upset.

2. Jason didn't <u>pick</u> the car <u>up</u> until after six o'clock.

3. Jason didn't <u>show up</u> at four o'clock to get his father because he was at the movie theater watching a film.

4. After Jason <u>dropped</u> the car <u>off</u> at the garage, he went to the movies.

5. Parents are responsible for <u>bringing up</u> their children.

B. Use a phrasal verb from the reading to answer each question below.

1. What did Jason do before he went to the theater?

   He dropped the car off at the garage.

2. Why did Jason's father call the garage?

   Because Jason didn't show up on time

3. Why did Jason's father feel like a failure?

   Because

Past perfect
Form: *had* + past participle

Meaning: The past perfect is used to show that one thing happened before another in the past.

*I drove up to the place where we **had planned** to meet.*
*Dad found out that I **had gone** to the movies.*

A. Complete the sentences below with the past perfect form of the verb in parentheses.

1. I knew Dad would be angry if he found out that

   I ___had gone___ (go) to the movies.

2. I told my father that it ___took___ (take) a lot

   longer to fix the car than we ___had expected___ (expect).

3. My father knew I was lying because he ___had___

   already ___called___ (call) the garage to find out if
   there was a problem.

4. My father felt that he ___had failed___ (fail) as a father.

5. I lied to my father when he asked me where

   I ___had been___ (be).

B. Simple past or past perfect? Underline the correct verb form in parentheses. Compare your answers with a partner's.

1. When I (arrived/had arrived) at our meeting place, I saw my father waiting patiently.

2. Jason picked up the car from the garage after he (saw/had seen) a couple of movies.

3. Dad walked down the dusty road and I (followed/had followed) behind him.

4. Dad knew I was lying because he (called/had called) the garage two hours before.

5. My father (believed/had believed) that he had failed as a father.

Discussion & Writing

A. Jason's father chose an interesting way to teach his son a lesson. What could parents do in the following situations to teach their children a lesson? Work in a group to come up with a suggestion for each situation.

1. "When I was about six years old, my mother left me at a friend's house for a few hours. This friend had a large supply of pens and pencils, and I took a few of them without telling her. Later my mother saw the pens and asked me where I got them. When I told her, she _____."

2. "In my family, we weren't allowed to use any bad words. Even telling someone to 'shut up' was against the rules. One time when I told my sister to shut up, my mother _____."

3. "I don't remember this, but my relatives tell me that when I was little, I took some chalk and drew pictures on the outside of the house. My grandfather was the first to see my pictures and he _____."

B. Follow the steps below to share stories with a partner.

1. Think about a time when you misbehaved[11] as a child. Then answer the questions below on another piece of paper.

   • How old were you?

   • Where were you?

   • How did you misbehave?

   • Why do you think you misbehaved?

2. Get together in a group. Take turns reading your answers aloud. For each situation, work together to decide how you think the parents should respond to the child's misbehavior.

---

[11] **misbehaved**   behaved badly

Crossword Puzzle

Use words from the reading to complete the crossword puzzle.

Across:

2 A synonym for the verb *fix* is ___.

7 Another word for *a chance to do something* is ___. (line 5)

9 The opposite of *succeeded* is ___.

10 The past tense of *drive* is ___.

12 A ___ is equal to 1.6 kilometers.

Down:

1 The past tense of *bring up* is ___ up.

3 The opposite of *remember* is ___.

4 When you ___ to someone, you say you are sorry. (line 17)

5 The past tense of *drop off* is ___ off.

6 Another word for *without noise* is ___. (line 39)

8 It is easy to lose ___ of time when you are having fun. (line 10)

11 The opposite of *drop off* is ___ up.

Chapter Goals

CONTENT:
Achieving academic success through teamwork

READING SKILL:
Skimming

BUILDING VOCABULARY:
Learning team-related words

LANGUAGE FOCUS:
Understanding subject gerunds

"It's in supporting one another that two hands find strength."

— *Abdiliaahi Muuse*
Somali sage
(1890 –1966)

2 Student Learning Teams

Before You Read

> *"A team is a small number of people with complementary skills[1] who are committed to a common purpose, set of goals, and approach."*—from the *Harvard Business Review*

1. Read the definition of a team above. Match the teams on the left with the goals on the right in the chart below.

TEAMS	GOALS
_____a. World Cup team	1. to save the lives of patients
_____b. software production team	2. to develop computer applications
_____c. team of doctors in an emergency room	3. to find and help lost or injured climbers
_____d. search and rescue team in the mountains	4. to compete in and win the soccer championship

2. What makes a team successful? Why are some teams more successful than others? Share your ideas with a partner.

3. Read the title of the article. Then look over the article quickly. What do you think the article will be about? Share your ideas with a partner.

---

[1] **complementary skills**   different abilities that strengthen the team

STUDENT LEARNING TEAMS

by John N. Gardner and A. Jerome Jewler

from *Your College Experience*

1   Research has shown that college students can learn as much, or more, from peers [2] as they do from instructors and textbooks. When students work effectively in a supportive group, the experience can be a very powerful way to improve academic achievement and
5   satisfaction with the learning experience.

Recent interviews with college students at **Harvard University** revealed that nearly every **senior** who had been part of a **study group** considered this experience crucial to his or her academic progress and success. The list below describes several important activities that
10 you and your study group or **learning team** can collaborate on:

Activities for a learning team

1. **Sharing class notes**. Team up with [3] other students immediately after class to share and compare notes. One of your teammates may have picked up [4] something you missed
15   or vice versa.[5]

2. **Comparing ideas about assigned readings**. After completing each week's readings, team up with other students to compare your **highlighting and margin notes**. See if you all agree on what the author's major points were and what
20   information in the chapter you should study for exams.

3. **Doing library research**. Studies show that many students are unfamiliar with library research and sometimes experience "library anxiety." Forming library research teams is an effective way to develop a social support group for
25   reducing this fear and for locating and sharing information.

---

[2] **peers**   classmates

[3] **team up with**   get together with

[4] **picked up**   understood

[5] **vice versa**   just the opposite, i.e., you may have picked up something your teammates missed

4. Meeting with the instructor. Having your team visit the instructor during **office hours** to seek additional assistance in preparing for exams is an effective team learning strategy for several reasons. If you are shy or unassertive, it may be easier to see an instructor in the company of other students. Your team visit also sends a message to the instructor that you are serious about learning.

5. Reviewing test results. After receiving test results, the members of a learning team can review their individual tests together to help one another identify the sources of their mistakes and to identify any "model" answers that received maximum credit. You can use this information to improve your performance on subsequent tests or assignments.

Not all learning teams, however, are equally effective. Sometimes group work is unsuccessful or fails to reach its full potential because insufficient thought was given to how teams should be formed or how they should function. The following suggestions are strategies for maximizing the power of peer collaboration.

1. In forming teams, seek peers who will contribute quality and diversity. Look for fellow students who are motivated: who attend class regularly, are attentive and participate actively while in class, and complete assignments on time.

Include teammates from both genders as well as students with different personality characteristics. Such variety will bring different life experiences and different styles of thinking and learning strategies to your team, which can increase both its quality and versatility.

Furthermore, choosing only your friends or classmates who have similar interests and lifestyles can often result in a learning group that is more likely to get off track[6] and onto topics that have nothing to do with the learning task.

2. Keep your group size small (three to six classmates). Smaller groups allow for more face-to-face interaction and eye contact and less opportunity for any one individual to shirk his or her responsibility.[7] Also, it's much easier for small groups to get together outside of class.

---

[6] **get off track**   become distracted or lose focus

[7] **shirk his or her responsibility**   not do the work he or she agreed to do

Consider choosing an even number of teammates, so you can work in pairs in case the team decides to divide its work into separate parts for different members to work on.

65 **3. Hold individual team members accountable for**[8] **contributing to the learning of their teammates**. Research on study groups at Harvard University indicates that they are effective only if each member has done the required course work in advance of the group meeting. One way to
70 ensure proper preparation is to ask each member to come to the group meeting prepared with specific information to share with teammates, as well as with questions on which they would like to receive help from the team.

Another way to ensure that each teammate prepares properly
75 for the meeting is to have individual members take on different roles or responsibilities. For example, each member could assume special responsibility for mastering a particular topic,[9] section, or skill to be taught to the others.

This course may be the perfect place for you to form learning teams
80 and to start putting principles of good teamwork into practice.[10] The teamwork skills you build in this course can be applied to your future courses, particularly those which you find most difficult. What's more, **national surveys** of employers consistently show that being able to work effectively in teams is one of the most important and valued
85 skills in today's work world.

About the Authors

John N. Gardner is professor of library and information science and **A. Jerome Jewler** is professor of journalism and mass communications at the University of South Carolina, Columbia. The authors specialize in helping students make a successful transition from high school to college.

---

[8] **hold someone accountable for**   make someone responsible for

[9] **mastering a particular topic**   becoming an expert in a specific subject area

[10] **putting principles into practice**   incorporating ideas and words into real-life actions

After You Read

A. True, False, or Impossible to Know? Read the statements below and write T (True), F (False), or I (Impossible to Know).

1. One of the main purposes of the reading is to encourage students to form learning teams. _____

2. In a recent study, virtually all Harvard University students said that joining a study team helped them be more successful. _____

3. According to the article, a team that includes men and women will probably be more effective than a team with only men. _____

4. To be successful, learning teams need a strong leader. _____

5. It's a good idea to form teams of people who have similar interests. _____

6. From the reading, you can infer that a team of five people is better than a team of six. _____

B. Consider the issues. Work with a partner to answer the questions below.

1. The authors describe several learning team activities that can improve your academic performance. Which team activity would help you most? Which activity would help you least? Why?

2. The reading provides information on what you *should* do to form and maintain an effective study team. Make a list of three to five things you *shouldn't* do when putting together and maintaining a learning team.

3. The authors say that teamwork is one of the most valued skills in today's work world. Why do you think this is true?

Skimming

When you skim a reading selection, you read it quickly to learn about its content and organization. You don't read every word. Instead, your eyes move very quickly over the selection, trying to find general information (e.g., the topic of a reading).

A. Read the two questions below. Then, take **one minute** to skim the reading below for the answers. Discuss your answers with a partner.

1. What is the topic of the following reading selection? _____

   _____

2. Who is the audience for this reading? _____

   _____

Getting Ready for the Message

from *Your College Experience*

Listening in class is not like listening to a TV program, listening to a friend, or even listening to a speaker at a meeting. The difference, of course, is that what is said in class is vital to your success in the class. Knowing how to listen can help you get more out of what you hear, understand better what you have heard, and save you time in the process. Here are eight strategies that will help you be a more effective listener in class:

1. **Be ready for the message**. Prepare yourself to hear, to listen, and to receive the message.

2. **Listen to the main concepts and central ideas**, not just to facts and figures. Although facts are important, they will be easier to remember when you place them in a context of concepts, themes, and ideas.

3. **Listen for new ideas.** Even if you are an expert on the topic, you can still learn something new. Assuming you have "already heard all this before" means that your mind will be closed to any new information.

4. **Really hear what is said.** Hearing "sounds" is not the same as hearing the intended message. Listening involves hearing what the speaker wants you to receive, to understand, and to learn.

5. **Repeat mentally.** Words that you hear can go in one ear and out the other unless you make an effort to retain them. Think about what you hear and make an active effort to retain it by repeating it silently to yourself.

6. **Think.** Decide whether you think what you have heard is important. Reflect on the new information.

7. **Ask questions.** If you did not hear or understand what was said, raise your hand! Now is the time to clarify things. Typically, one student will ask a question that many students in the room are wondering about.

8. **Sort, organize, and categorize.** When you listen, try to match what you are hearing with your previous knowledge. Take an active role in deciding how you want to recall what you are learning.

B. Now, share your answers with a partner. Was it difficult to answer the two questions in **A** above in only one minute? How can skimming help you become a more effective reader?

Building Vocabulary

Learning team-related words and phrases
When you learn one new word, you can often expand your vocabulary by using your dictionary to find related words and expressions.

A. Read the team-related words and phrases below. Use your dictionary to find the meaning of any words and phrases you don't know. Then add one or two more team-related words.

TEAM-RELATED WORDS AND PHRASES

Verbs	*Nouns*
team up	teammate
form a team	team work
be on a team	team approach
_____	_____

B. Choose a team-related word from the chart on page 19 to complete the quotations below. In some cases there is more than one possible answer.

1. "I enjoy working with all five of my _____. Each one brings different skills and experiences to the group."

2. "We usually _____ after class to share notes and talk about the most important ideas that the professor mentioned."

3. "Some of my friends like to study on their own, but I prefer a _____ to studying for tests and working on research projects."

4. "My learning team was always getting off track, so we decided to choose a _____ to organize and coordinate our meetings."

5. "I know that I'll be able to apply the _____ skills I learn in this course to my first job after college."

6. "I'm really glad that my professor asked three of my classmates and me to _____. My grades have really improved after only a month of studying together."

Language Focus

Understanding subject gerunds
A **gerund** or **gerund** phrase can be the subject of a sentence. We often use subject gerunds to state our opinions or to make our writing more persuasive. Subject gerunds always take a singular verb.

Collaborating with your peers can improve your academic performance.

Having your team visit the instructor is an effective team learning strategy.

A. Change the verb in **boldface** to a gerund. Then rewrite each of the sentences below so that it begins with a subject gerund.

Example
It's relatively easy for small groups of students to **get** together outside of class.

Getting together outside of class is relatively easy for small groups of students.

1. An important thing to remember when forming a team is to **find** fellow students who are bright and motivated.

   _____

   _____

2. An effective way to divide the work on a large research project is to **form** library research teams.

   _____

   _____

3. If you are shy, it may be easier to **see** an instructor in the company of other students.

   _____

   _____

4. It's every team member's responsibility to **make** sure each individual does his or her work.

   _____

   _____

5. It's a good idea to **team** up with other students before an exam to review lecture notes.

   _____

   _____

B. Complete the sentences below with your own ideas. Then, share your work with a partner.

1. Being part of a learning team _____

   _____ .

2. Working with students I don't know _____

   _____ .

3. Studying at an American university _____

   _____ .

4. Becoming a fluent speaker of English _____

   _____ .

5. Falling in love _____

   _____ .

6. Having children _____

_____.

Discussion & Writing

"Great discoveries and improvements involve the cooperation of many minds."

— Alexander Graham Bell, Scottish
inventor (1847 – 1922)

"The total is often greater than the sum of the parts."

— American expression

"When spiderwebs unite, they can tie up a lion."

— Ethiopian proverb

1. What do the quotations above mean to you? How does each one relate to ideas in this chapter?

2. Forming a student learning team is one effective way to improve your academic success. What are some other things you can do to improve your academic performance?

3. Form a learning team in this class with a small group of students. Follow as many of the suggestions in this chapter as possible. After one month, tell your classmates about the advantages and disadvantages of working on a learning team.

Crossword Puzzle

Use words from the reading to complete the crossword puzzle.

Across:

1 We sometimes call a teacher an ___. (line 2)

3 It's important to ___ classes regularly.

5 Another word for *fear* is ___. (line 23)

7 The word ___ means *in addition*. (line 53)

11 The opposite of *false* is ___.

12 The plural form of *activity* is ___.

15 The word ___. is similar in meaning to 7 across.

16 my, ___, his, her, our

17 Another word for a *test* is an ___.

Down:

2 Students in their last year of high school or university are called ___.

3 The opposite of *before* is ___.

4 An ___ person listens very carefully. (line 46)

6 The past tense of *choose* is ___.

8 The ___ score on most tests is 100. (line 37)

9 A word for *very important* is ___. (line 8)

10 The opposite of *minor* is ___.

13 A group of people working together is called a ___. (line 11)

14 A ___ person doesn't feel comfortable meeting new people.

CONTENT:
Adjusting to life in a foreign country

READING SKILL:
Understanding the difference between topic and main idea

BUILDING VOCABULARY:
Learning expressions with *feel*

LANGUAGE FOCUS:
Comparing *used to, get used to,* and *be used to*

> "*Culture is everything. Culture is the way we dress, the way we carry our heads, the way we walk, the way we tie our ties.*"

— *Aimé Zesair*
French writer
(1913 –   )

Chapter ▲ 3 Culture Shock

Before You Read

1. "Culture shock" is a popular term used to talk about how people react when they are in foreign places. What do you think it means?

2. Read the title of the article on pages 26–28 and then take one minute to skim it. What do you think the article will be about? Share your ideas with a partner.

3. In this reading, an Australian student compares life in Australia with life in the United States. As you read, take notes in the chart below on some of the differences this student talks about.

TOPIC	AUSTRALIA	THE UNITED STATES
1. Driving	Less traffic than in the US; steering wheel on right side	Crazy drivers; more traffic than in Australia
2. Pace of life		
3. Drinking alcohol		
4. Relationships between professors and students		

CULTURE SHOCK

by Bob Weinstein

from *The Boston Globe*

1   Saying Tamara Blackmore experienced **culture shock** when she
arrived here last September is an understatement. It was more like
culture trauma[1] for this adventurous student who left **Melbourne**'s
Monash University to spend her junior year at **Boston College** (BC).
5   Blackmore, 20, was joined at BC by 50 other **exchange students**
from around the world. Like the thousands of exchange students who
enroll in American colleges each year, Blackmore discovered
firsthand[2] there is a sea of difference[3] between reading about and
experiencing America firsthand. She felt the difference as soon as she
10   stepped off the plane.

As soon as she landed in **Boston**, Blackmore could feel the tension
in the air. She was about to taste a lifestyle[4] far more hectic than the
one she left. "Driving in Boston is crazy," says Blackmore. "It took me
a while to get used to the roads and the driving style here. I was
15   always afraid someone was going to hit me. It was particularly tricky
since the steering wheel was on the wrong side of the car. In
Australia, it's on the right side." Beyond the cars and traffic jams,
Blackmore said it took a while to get used to so many people in one
place, all of whom seemed like they were moving at warp speed.[5]

20   "There are only 18 million people in **Australia** spread out over an
entire country," she says, "compared to more than six million people in
the state of **Massachusetts** alone. We don't have the kind of congestion
you have in Boston. There is a whole different perception of space."

The pressing problem for Blackmore was making a quick adjustment
25   to the American lifestyle that felt like it was run by a stopwatch. For
this easygoing Australian, Americans seemed like perpetual-motion
machines.[6] "Americans are very time-oriented," Blackmore says.

---

[1] **culture trauma**   extreme form of "culture shock"
[2] **discovered firsthand**   learned by directly seeing or
experiencing
[3] **sea of difference**   very big difference
[4] **taste a lifestyle**   experience a way of life
[5] **moving at warp speed**   traveling very, very quickly
[6] **perpetual-motion machines**   machines that never stop moving

"Everything is done according to a schedule. They're always busy, which made me feel guilty about wanting to just sit around and occasionally watch television. Australians, on the other hand, value their leisure time. The pace there is a lot slower because we don't feel the need to always be busy. It's not that Australians are lazy, it's just that they have a different concept of how time should be spent. Back home, I used to spend a lot more time just talking to my friends."

It didn't take long for Blackmore to adjust to American rhythms.[7] "I felt the pressure to work harder and do more because everyone was running around doing so much," she says. When BC students weren't huddled over books, Blackmore found it odd that they were compulsively jogging, running, biking, or doing aerobics in order to be thin. "Compared to home, the girls here are very skinny," she says. "Before I got here, I heard a lot of stories about the pressure to be thin and that many young American women have **eating disorders**. I'll go out with a friend and just tuck into a good meal[8] and have a good time, whereas an American girl would just pick at her food.[9]"

When it comes to drinking, Blackmore says Australians have a lot more freedom. "We're more casual about drinking at home," she says, "whereas there are many rules and regulations attached to when and where you can drink in the United States," not to mention a **legal drinking age of 21** compared with Australia's legal drinking age of 18.

But it's BC's laid-back[10] and friendly learning environment that sets it apart from her Melbourne college experience. "Generally speaking, learning facilities are a lot better in Boston," she says. "In Australia, students and teachers have little contact outside the classroom. It's a formal and depersonalized relationship. College is a place you go for a few hours every day and then go home. Your social life and school life are separate."

It's just the opposite at BC, according to Blackmore. "BC students and faculty are like one big happy family," she says. "There is a real sense of team spirit. It's like we're all in this together. Going to school here is a lifestyle, whereas at home we're just a number. We attend school to get a degree so we can graduate, get a job, and get on with our lives.[11]"

---

[7] **adjust to American rhythms**   get used to American lifestyles
[8] **tuck into a good meal**   enjoy a meal (Australian expression)
[9] **pick at her food**   eat only a small amount of food on her plate
[10] **laid-back**   relaxed
[11] **get on with our lives**   move ahead in our lives

Another pleasant shocker[12] was the close and open relationships
65 American students enjoy with their teachers. It's a sharp contrast to
Australia, where college students keep a discreet but respectful
distance from their teachers. "I was surprised when I learned
students go out to dinner with their lecturers," she says. "We just
don't do that back home. Professors deal with hundreds of students
70 and you're lucky if they remember your name."

When Blackmore returns to Australia at the end of the school year,
she'll have plenty of memories, most of them good ones. BC, like most
American colleges, has gone out of its way to create a memorable
experience for Blackmore and its other exchange students.

About the Author

Bob Weinstein is a New York journalist who writes *Tech Watch*, a
weekly syndicated column. He wrote this article for **The Boston
Globe**, a major daily newspaper in Boston, Massachusetts, in the
United States.

After You Read

Understanding the Text

A. Multiple choice. For each item below, circle the **two** answers that
best complete each statement.

1. The purpose of the reading is to _____.
   a. demonstrate that Americans study hard and exercise a lot
   b. show one student's thoughts on cultural differences between
   Australia and the United States
   c. point out some ways in which foreigners experience culture
   shock in the United States
   d. argue that everyone should spend a year as a foreign exchange
   student

---

[12] **shocker**   surprise

2. Tamara Blackmore says that _____ in Australia.

    a. students and teachers sometimes become good friends

    b. students make a clear separation between their academic and social lives

    c. professors often do not know their students' names

    d. universities are not as good

3. Blackmore says that American professors _____ their students.

    a. have dinner with

    b. enjoy warm relationships with

    c. jog, run, and bike with

    d. are smarter than

4. When it comes to drinking alcohol, Blackmore feels that _____.

    a. there are stricter rules in America than in Australia

    b. the drinking age in Australia is too low

    c. Americans drink more than Australians

    d. Australians are more relaxed about alcohol than Americans

5. Blackmore would probably agree that _____.

    a. Americans are better drivers than Australians

    b. American professors take a greater interest in their students than Australian professors

    c. Australians are more relaxed than Americans

    d. American women enjoy good food more than Australian women

6. The overall tone of the reading is _____ and _____.

    a. humorous

    b. thoughtful

    c. upsetting

    d. informative

B. Consider the issues. Work with a partner to answer the questions below.

1. Tell your partner about three differences Tamara sees between life in Australia and the United States.

   *"**Tamara says that** the drivers in Boston are crazy. **She says that** there is more traffic congestion in Boston than in Australia. **Also, Tamara mentions that** the steering wheel is on the right side of the car in Australia, but on the wrong side in the United States. **She means that** the steering wheel is on the left side in American cars."*

2. Tamara noticed many cultural differences between Australia and the United States. Which cultural differences do you think were relatively easy for Tamara to get used to? Which ones do you think were difficult? Why?

3. From what Tamara says, do you think that university life in your country is more similar to university life in Australia or the United States? Why?

Reading Skill

Understanding the difference between topic and main idea

A **topic** is the subject or general idea of a piece of writing. A **main idea** is the writer's message about the topic. Typically, writers organize their writing around one or two main ideas.

Example from Chapter 2

> **Topic**
> Student learning teams
>
> **Main idea**
> Forming a learning team can improve your academic performance.

A. Topic and main idea of a paragraph. Read the paragraph below and find the topic and main idea. Discuss your answers with a partner.

Many visitors to the United States think that Americans take their exercise and free time activities too seriously. Americans often schedule their recreation as if they were scheduling business appointments. They go jogging every day at the same time, play tennis two or three times a week, or swim every Thursday. Foreigners often think that this kind of recreation sounds more like work than relaxation. For many Americans, however, their recreational activities are relaxing and enjoyable, or at least worthwhile, because they contribute to health and physical fitness.

—adapted from *American Ways:*
A Guide for Foreigners in the United States
by Gary Althen

1. The topic of this paragraph is:
   a. Health and fitness
   b. Popular recreational activities in the United States
   c. The American approach to recreation

2. The main idea of this paragraph is:
   a. Jogging, tennis, and swimming are popular American sports.
   b. There are many effective ways to exercise well and stay healthy.
   c. Americans enjoy their structured and organized approach to recreation.

B. Topic and main idea of a longer selection. Look back at the reading on pages 28–30 and find the topic and main idea. Discuss your answers with a partner.

1. The topic of the reading is:
   a. Experiencing culture shock in the United States
   b. The definition and theory of culture shock
   c. Social life at Boston College

2. The main idea of the reading is:

   a. There are many cultural differences between life in Australia and life in the United States.

   b. Everyone experiences culture shock when they move from one country to another.

   c. Students at Boston College are very time-oriented because they have a lot to do.

Building Vocabulary

Learning new expressions
When you see a new expression, pay careful attention to the sentence you find it in. The sentence can give you clues about the meaning of the expression and help you remember it.

A. In the chart below are five expressions with *feel* that are used in the reading. Below each expression write the sentence in which it appears in the reading.

1. feel the difference

_____

_____

2. feel the tension

_____

_____

3. feel like

_____

_____

4. feel guilty

_____

_____

5. feel the pressure

_____

_____

B. Discuss your answers to the following questions with a partner.

1. When was the last time you felt tension in the air? Where were you? What was happening?

2. Which of the following situations would make you feel the guiltiest? Why?

a. lying to your mother or father

b. forgetting a friend's birthday

c. borrowing something and accidentally breaking it

Language Focus

Comparing <u>used to</u>, <u>get used to</u> and <u>be used to</u>

Used to refers to things done on a regular basis in the past, but no longer done in the present.

*Back home, I **used to** spend a lot more time just talking to my friends.*

Get used to means to become accustomed to something new.

*It took me a while to **get used to** the roads and the driving style in Boston.*

Be used to means to be comfortable with something.

*For six months, Tamara had a difficult time adjusting to American customs. Now she **is used to** living in the United States.*

A. Read the sentences. Then write if each statement that follows is T (True) or F (False).

1. It took a while for Tamara to *get used to living* in a big city like Boston.

When Tamara first moved to Boston, she wasn't comfortable living there. _____

2. Ellen *used to believe* in love at first sight.

Ellen doesn't believe in love at first sight now. _____

3. When Alice was a child, she *used to visit* her grandparents every summer.

As a child, Alice seldom visited her grandparents in the summer. _____

4. John has had his own apartment for five years, so he *is used to living* alone.

John is accustomed to living alone. _____

5. Though I lived in Mexico for many years, I never *got used to* the spicy food.

These days, the speaker enjoys spicy food. _____

B. Write down three things that you **used to do**, three things that are hard to **get used to**, and three things that you are **used to doing** on your own. Share your answers with a partner.

Discussion & Writing

1. Based on Tamara Blackmore's comments in the reading, would you rather study for a year in Australia or the United States? Why?

2. Imagine that Tamara was coming to your country to study for a year. What advice would you give her? What would you tell her about the food, the students, the professors, and other aspects of university life in your country?

3. Have you ever experienced culture shock? Describe your experience. Which country were you in? How long were you there? What are your most positive and negative memories of the experience?

4. Think of a country where you would like to study or work for six months to a year. What would you do to prepare for living in this country? Make a list of five questions you have about life in this country and research the answers to these questions.

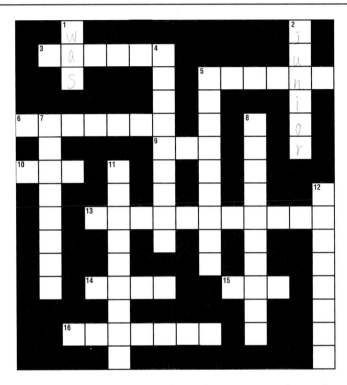

Use words from the reading to complete the crossword puzzle.

Across:

3 The opposite of *formal* is ___.

5 A *very thin* person can be described as ___. (line 40)

6 Your free time is also called your ___ time. (line 31)

9 When you get tired of standing, you can ___ in a chair.

10 In the United States, the legal drinking ___ is 21.

13 ___ means work together with one or more people. (Ch. 2, line 10)

14 Before an airplane can ___, the pilot must put the wheels down.

15 The opposite of *little* is ___.

16 The teaching staff at a university is called the ___. (line 59)

Down:

1 The past form of *am* is ___.

2 Your third year in high school or university is called your ___ year. (line 4)

4 The way you live is called your ___. (line 12)

5 The ninth month in a year is called ___.

7 In Australia you can drink alcohol when you are ___ years old.

8 A person from Australia is an ___.

11 A handheld instrument used to time something is called a ___. (line 25)

12 According to Blackmore, social life and school life in Australia are ___. (line 57)

> "*The same person cannot be skilled in everything; each has his special excellence.*"
>
> —Euripides
> Greek playwright
> (c. 485 – 406 BC)

Chapter ▲ **4** A Young Blind Whiz

Before You Read

1. Read the title of the article on pages 38–39 and then take one minute to skim it. What do you think the article will be about? Share your ideas with a partner.

2. There are many computer-related words in the article on pages 38–39. Before you read the article, answer the questions with a partner.

   a. A *laptop* is an example of computer hardware. So is a *mainframe*. What other examples of computer hardware can you think of?

   b. Describe what these computer parts are for: *screen, keyboard, mouse.*

   c. What types of computer *software* have you used?

   d. A *network* is a group of connected computers. What do you think the advantages of a computer network are?

3. Read the first paragraph of the article on the next page. What would you like to find out about Suleyman Gokyigit? Write three questions. Then read the article to find the answers to your questions.

   Example: *What does he do on computers?*

   1. _____

   2. _____

   3. _____

A YOUNG, BLIND WHIZ[1] ON COMPUTERS

by Tom Petzinger

from *The Wall Street Journal*

1   Sometimes, a perceived disability [2] turns out to be an asset on the job. Though he is only 18 years old and blind, Suleyman Gokyigit (pronounced gok-yi-it) is among the top computer technicians and programmers at InteliData Technologies Corp., a large software
5   company with several offices across the United States.

      "After a merger [3] last October, two disparate computer networks [4] were driving us crazy," recalls Douglas Braun, an InteliData vice president. "We couldn't even send e-mail to each other." In three weeks, Mr. Gokyigit, a University of Toledo **sophomore** who **works**
10   **part-time** at InteliData's office in the city, created the software needed to integrate the two networks. "None of the company's 350 other employees could have done the job in three months," says Mr. Braun. "Suleyman can literally 'see' into the heart of the computer."

      Mr. Gokyigit's gift, as Mr. Braun calls it, is an unusual ability to
15   conceptualize[5] the innards[6] of a machine. "The computer permits me to reach out into the world and do almost anything I want to do," says Mr. Gokyigit, who is a computer science engineering major with **straight As**.

      Like most blind people who work with computers, Mr. Gokyigit
20   uses a voice-synthesizer that reads the video display on his monitor in a mechanical voice. Devices that produce **Braille** screen displays are also available, but Mr. Gokyigit says they "waste time." Instead, he depends on memory. Turning the synthesizer to top speed, he remembers almost everything he hears, at least until a project is
25   completed. While the synthesizer talks, Mr. Gokyigit mentally "maps" the computer screen with numbered coordinates (such as three

---

[1] **whiz**   very talented person

[2] **a perceived disability**   something you think of as a disability or negative thing

[3] **merger**   a combining of two or more companies into one

[4] **two disparate computer networks**   two groups of computers that can't communicate with each other

[5] **to conceptualize**   to form an idea of

[6] **the innards of**   the inside of

across, two down) and memorizes the location of each icon on the grid[7] so he can call up files with his mouse.

The young programmer is also at home with[8] hardware, thanks partly to a highly developed sense of touch. Mitzi Nowakowski, an office manager at InteliData, recalls how he easily disconnected and reconnected their computer systems during a move last year. "Through feel, Suleyman can locate[9] connectors, pins and wires much faster than most other people with sight," she says.

Several months ago, on a trip to San Francisco, Mr. Braun had difficulty accessing[10] the company's mainframe using his laptop. He needed specific numbers to get into four InteliData files. Instead of asking someone to manually search a thick logbook[11] of computer addresses, he called Mr. Gokyigit, who had committed the logbook to memory and produced the proper numbers "in ten seconds," Mr. Braun says.

Much of the student programmer's speed comes from his ability to block out[12] distractions while at the computer. When typing, he listens intently to the synthesizer. His long, thin fingers fly over the keyboard. "Nothing seems to shake his concentration," says Mrs. Nowakowski, his immediate boss.[13]

Mr. Gokyigit is the only company employee on call[14] 24 hours a day. "We consider him our top troubleshooter,[15]" says Mr. Braun.

About the Author

Tom Petzinger has worked for *The Wall Street Journal* as a columnist, editor and reporter for over 20 years. *The Wall Street Journal* is the leading business publication in the United States. It includes stock quotes, national and international business news and trends, and features articles such as this one on interesting people in the world of business.

---

[7] **grid**   a pattern of evenly spaced vertical and horizontal lines

[8] **at home with**   comfortable with; good with

[9] **locate**   find the position of

[10] **accessing**   getting into; getting information from

[11] **logbook**   written record of information

[12] **block out**   ignore

[13] **his immediate boss**   the person he reports directly to

[14] **on call**   available to go to work

[15] **troubleshooter**   problem solver

After You Read

Understanding the Text

A. True or False? Read the statements about Suleyman Gokyigit and write T (True) or F (False). Then correct the statements that are not true.

  F   **1.** He uses a ~~Braille screen display~~ to read the video display *(voice-synthesizer)* on his computer monitor.

_____ **2.** He is in his second year at the university and he is majoring in computer science engineering.

_____ **3.** He is an excellent student.

_____ **4.** He is on call twelve hours a day.

_____ **5.** He was able to help the vice-president locate a computer address because he keeps all the addresses in his logbook.

_____ **6.** He can solve both hardware and software problems.

B. Consider the issues. Work with a partner to answer the questions below.

1. Choose three adjectives to describe Suleyman Gokyigit. Then tell why you chose each word.

ADJECTIVES	REASONS
1.	
2.	
3.	

2. What are Suleyman's talents and abilities?

3. What can Suleyman do better than those with sight?

4. In addition to computer programming, what jobs do you think Suleyman would be good at? Why?

Inferencing

An **inference** is a logical conclusion drawn from evidence.

Evidence	**Inference**
Your friend is crying.	*Your friend is sad.* OR
	Your friend just got some bad news.

Evidence	**Inference**
You friend is in the	*Your friend is not well.* OR
hospital.	*Your friend had an accident.*

A. Match the **Evidence** with one or more logical **Inferences**. Write the numbers in the blanks on the right.

EVIDENCE	INFERENCES
1. Your friend doesn't answer the phone.	_____ Your friend is thirsty.
	_____ Your friend isn't hungry.
2. You see your friend drink several glasses of water.	_____ Your friend is going somewhere special.
3. Your friend doesn't want to eat anything for lunch.	_____ Your friend isn't at home.
4. Your friend is dressed nicely.	_____ Your friend doesn't feel well.

B. What can you infer about Suleyman Gokyigit from the **Evidence** below? Check (√) one or more ideas. Compare your answers with a partner.

1. Evidence: Mr. Gokyigit is a straight-A student in computer science engineering.

_____ He is smart. _____ He has a lot of money.

_____ He is a good student. _____ He has always gotten good grades.

2. Evidence: Mr. Gokyigit learned all of the computer addresses in the company's thick logbook.

_____ He wrote the logbook. _____ He has a good memory.

_____ It's easy for anyone to learn the logbook. _____ It was easy for him to learn the addresses.

3. Evidence: In three weeks, Mr. Gokyigit created the software needed at InteliData. "None of the company's 350 other employees could have done the job in three months," says Mr. Braun.

_____ The company's 350 other employees are lazy.

_____ Gokyigit works very fast.

_____ Gokyigit only worked for InteliData for three weeks.

_____ No one else at InteliData could do the job.

Building Vocabulary

Compound nouns: noun + noun
The names for some things are made up of two nouns. The first noun is usually singular even when the second noun is plural.

mousepad   _computer programs_   _voice-synthesizers_

A. Create a compound noun using two nouns from the box below to complete each sentence. The compound noun might be one word, two words, or hyphenated.

office	work	synthesizer	programmers
book	top	computer	manager
video	net	lap	log

1. Many computers connected to each other are called a computer

   _____.

2. A _____ - _____ reads a video display in a mechanical voice.

3. Mitzi Nowakowski's job at InteliData is

   _____ _____.

4. New software is created each day by

   _____ _____.

5. A _____ is a portable computer sometimes only the size of a book.

6. Suleyman had committed InteliData's thick

   _____ full of computer addresses to memory.

B. Find a compound noun in the article on pages 38–39 to complete each sentence below.

1. You need a _____ to type words into a computer.

2. Because Suleyman is so skilled at locating problems and solving them, he is respected as the company's number one _____ .

3. Suleyman's major at the University of Toledo is _____ _____ engineering.

4. Suleyman is considered among the best _____ _____ and programmers at his company.

5. Although Braille _____ _____ are available, Suleyman prefers to use a voice-synthesizer.

Language Focus

Reduced Clauses
We often shorten a clause with the pronouns *who*, *which*, or *that* when followed by the verbs *is*, *are*, *was* and *were*. Simply omit the pronoun and the verb *to be*.

Mitzi Nowakowski, **who is an office manager at InteliData,** *works with Mr. Gokyigit. = Mitzi Nowakowski,* **an office manager at InteliData***, works with Mr. Gokyigit.*

Gokyigit prefers the voice-synthesizer to the Braille screen displays **that are used to help the blind read with their fingertips.** *= Gokyigit prefers the voice-synthesizer to the Braille screen displays* **used to help the blind read with their fingertips.**

Cross out words to create a reduced clause. The first one is done for you.

1. Suleyman Gokyigit is one of the top computer technicians at InteliData Technologies Corp., ~~which is~~ a large software company.

2. InteliData, which is an American company, has about 350 employees.

3. Mr. Gokyigit, who is a University of Toledo sophomore, works part-time at InteliData's office in the city.

4. Two computer networks that were developed for disparate systems drove the managers of InteliData crazy.

5. "After a merger last October, two disparate computer networks were driving us crazy," recalls Douglas Braun, who is an InteliData vice president.

6. "The computer permits me to reach out into the world and do almost anything I want to do," says Mr. Gokyigit, who is a computer science engineering major.

Discussion & Writing

A. What do these quotations mean to you? How does each one relate to the ideas in the reading?

> *"If you cannot accomplish a thing, leave it and pass to[16] another which you can accomplish."*—Al Kali (901 – 967)
>
> *"It is not enough to have a good mind. The main thing is to use it well."*—René Descartes (1596 – 1650)
>
> *"If I have made any valuable discoveries, it has been owing more to[17] patient attention than to any other talent."*—Isaac Newton (1642 – 1727)

B. What are your partner's talents and abilities? Add one or two questions to the chart below. Then interview your partner and check (√) your partner's answers.

ARE YOU...	YES	NO	DO YOU HAVE...	YES	NO
good with numbers?	☐	☐	a good memory?	☐	☐
good at fixing things?	☐	☐	good balance?	☐	☐
a good typist?	☐	☐	a good voice?	☐	☐
a good public speaker?	☐	☐	a good imagination?	☐	☐
well organized?	☐	☐	good concentration?	☐	☐
_____	☐	☐	_____	☐	☐

Based on your partner's answers, in what profession do you think your partner could best use his or her talents?

---

[16] **pass to**   move to

[17] **owing more to**   due more to

Crossword Puzzle

Use words from the reading to complete the crossword puzzle.

Across:

1 A second-year university student is called a ___. (line 9)

4 A voice-synthesizer ___ the video display on a computer.

8 Another word for the *best* is the ___. (line 3)

9 A synonym for the adjective *correct* is ___. (line 40)

12 A ___ is someone who solves problems. (line 48)

15 Something that is very helpful to you is an ___ not a liability. (line 1)

17 To remember something, you must ___ it to memory. (line 39)

18 The opposite of *under* is ___.

Down:

1 A blind person cannot ___ the video display.

2 There are 24 ___ in a day.

3 A ___ takes place when two companies become one. (line 6)

5 The video display is part of a computer ___. (line 20)

6 People talking can be a ___ when you are watching a movie or studying. (line 43)

7 A voice synthesizer does not sound natural; it sounds ___. (line 21)

10 To function, a computer needs both hardware and ___. (line 4)

11 A ___ is made up of vertical and horizontal lines that cross each other. (line 28)

13 A synonym for *big* is ___.

14 Another word for a *talent* is a ___. (line 14)

Chapter Focus

CONTENT:
Music and copyright issues

READING SKILL:
Scanning

BUILDING VOCABULARY:
Grouping words

LANGUAGE FOCUS:
Present perfect

"Music is your own experience, your thoughts, your wisdom. If you don't live it, it won't come out of your horn."

— Charlie Parker
American jazz saxophonist
(1920 – 1955)

Chapter **5** Pop Group's Use of Folk Song Stirs Debate

Chapter ▲

Before You Read

1. What are some examples of traditional music from your country? Do you like this type of music?

2. Read the transcript, or written version, of the radio interview on pages 48–50 quickly. What is the name of the interviewer?

3. Read the first paragraph of the transcript on the next page. What questions does it raise for you? Write two more questions (Q) in the chart below. Then read the rest of the transcript and write answers (A) to the questions.

QUESTIONS AND ANSWERS
1. Q: Who sold the recording of Lee Fong Gwo's voice to the German musicians?
A:
2. Q: What's the name of the pop song with Lee Fong Gwo's voice?
A:
3. Q:
A:
4. Q:
A:

POP GROUP'S USE OF FOLK
SONG STIRS DEBATE[1]

from *National Public Radio*

1   Over the past decade, combining **traditional music** from Africa,
    Latin America, and Asia with Western pop[2] and **jazz** has become
    commonplace.[3] But for a singer of traditional music, having your
    voice on a hit record[4] does not necessarily make you any money.
5   Take the case of[5] Lee Fong Gwo, a Taiwanese rice farmer. His
    performance of a traditional song was recorded and later sold
    without his knowledge to a group of German pop musicians.
    The German musicians used the farmer's voice in a song that
    became a big hit. All this has stirred an interesting debate: Who
10 owns traditional music and should Lee Fong Gwo be paid for his
    performance?

FRANK KOLLER, REPORTER: For thousands of years, Lee Fong Gwo's
family has made a living growing rice in the mountains of southern
Taiwan. Gwo is an Ami; his ancestors came to Taiwan from the
15 islands of Southeast Asia long before Chinese immigrants arrived
from the mainland. Now 76, Lee Fong Gwo remembers learning to
sing in these fields as a young boy.

LEE FONG GWO, AMI SINGER: [through a translator] Our water
buffaloes needed someone to take care of them, and that was my job
20 until I was 12. In those days, I'd hear my whole family singing
together as they worked in the rice paddies,[6] and that's how I first
learned the songs.

FRANK KOLLER: A few miles away in the town of Taitung, you still see
traces of[7] traditional Ami culture in Lee Fong Gwo's garage. We spent
25 the afternoon sitting on small plastic chairs around a wok[8] filled with

---

[1] **stirs debate**   gets people talking about an issue

[2] **Western pop**   popular music from North America and Europe

[3] **commonplace**   ordinary

[4] **a hit record**   a very successful record

[5] **take the case of**   consider the example of

[6] **rice paddies**   wet land where rice is grown

[7] **traces of**   signs of; examples of

[8] **a wok**   a large pan that is shaped like a bowl

burning charcoal until Lee Fong Gwo asked me if I'd like to hear him and his wife sing one of the old songs.

Lee Fong Gwo and his wife sing a traditional song which fades[9] *into the pop song "Return to Innocence"*

30 This song, "Return to Innocence," was recorded by the German band Enigma in 1994. "Return to Innocence" sold more than five million copies around the world that year, staying on the **pop charts** for more than six months. The man whose unique chanting starts and ends "Return to Innocence," Lee Fong Gwo, was never asked to be on 35 the record and never received a cent[10]—and that was never supposed to happen, says Professor Hsu Chang-Wei, an ethnomusicologist[11] at Taiwan University.

In 1987, with support from the Taiwanese government and the French Ministry of Culture, Hsu arranged for a group of Ami singers led by 40 Lee Fong Gwo to visit Europe for a series of concerts.

PROFESSOR HSU CHANG-WEI, ETHNOMUSICOLOGIST, TAIWAN UNIVERSITY: [through a translator] In France, academics really liked the music and suggested that the performance be recorded. At that time, it was very rare to have Taiwanese ethnic music performed 45 outside of Taiwan. It was agreed that the Ami singer could be recorded and published in France, but just one CD for academic research purposes only.

FRANK KOLLER: The problem was, no one ever asked the Ami singers. In 1992, the musicians of Enigma heard the CD and 50 purchased—from the French Ministry of Culture—what they assumed were the complete rights[12] to use Lee Fong Gwo's voice. Enigma paid $6,000. The problem was, once again, no one asked Lee Fong Gwo.

LEE FONG GWO: Two years ago, my granddaughter brought a tape 55 home and played me the song on the Enigma record. That's the first time I heard that Enigma had used my voice. I was very surprised and happy. It felt good to have people using my voice, but I was also surprised because I never sang such a song with all those other sounds, and I wondered how it was made.

---

[9] **fades into**   slowly changes into
[10] **never received a cent**   didn't get any money
[11] **ethnomusicologist**   someone who studies traditional music
[12] **complete rights**   full legal permission

Frank Koller: When Ami leaders learned the story of Lee Fong Gwo's chanting on "Return to Innocence," they wrote to Enigma in Germany. The band replied that since a legal contract had been signed with the French government, no further payments would be made. For its part, the French Ministry of Culture has not responded and Robin Lee, the director of Taiwan's Association of Copyright Owners, says there's little chance for appeal.[13] Lee says the copyright[14] for a piece of music belongs to its composer, but a rice farmer such as Lee Fong Gwo does not qualify.

Robin Lee, Director, Taiwan Association of Copyright Owners: Because traditional music, by definition, is passed down from generation to generation over hundreds of years, we have lost who the original author is. It doesn't just simply follow that anyone who performs traditional music owns the copyright for it. This is not music that belongs to Lee Fong Gwo. It is his culture's music. It can't belong to one man.

Frank Koller: But the Ami do believe that the music belongs to Lee Fong Gwo. In fact, because Lee Fong Gwo is one of the oldest members of the tribe, they believe he is the music[15] and so does Professor Hsu Chang-Wei, the ethnomusicologist.

Hsu Chang-Wei: It's really more a moral issue than a legal one. In cases like this, copyrights should apply to the tribal peoples themselves. If Enigma has indeed made a lot of money from using this tribal music, then it's as if they were taking a treasure right from the tribe. They should pay something for that.

About the Source

National Public Radio (NPR) serves over 500 radio stations in the United States. Since NPR is commercial-free, it relies on government funds as well as donations from corporations and listeners. National Public Radio features news programs, interviews, classical and jazz music, and other types of cultural programs.

---

[13] **for appeal** for a legal review

[14] **copyright** ownership

[15] **he is the music** he has kept the music alive

After You Read

Understanding the Text

A. Multiple choice. For each item below, circle the best answer.

1. The main purpose of this interview was to _____.

   a. get people to buy the music of the group Enigma

   b. introduce people to Ami music

   c. discuss a moral and legal issue

   d. compare traditional and pop music

2. In line 44, the word "rare" means _____.

   a. cooked for a short time

   b. unusual

   c. thin

   d. reddish

3. You can infer from the text that Lee Fong Gwo _____.

   a. is a talented singer

   b. doesn't sing anymore

   c. has met the pop group Enigma

   d. wants to go back to France

4. Which event happened first?

   a. Enigma paid the French Ministry of Culture $6,000.

   b. The musicians of Enigma heard Lee Fong Gwo's recording.

   c. Lee Fong Gwo heard the song "Return to Innocence."

   d. Lee Fong Gwo traveled to Europe.

5. According to the interview, the pop group Enigma _____.

   a. studied folk singing in Taiwan

   b. communicated with several Ami singers before using the recording

   c. sold more than a million copies of "Return to Innocence" in 1994

   d. apologized to Lee Fong Gwo

6. The tone of this interview is _____.

   a. serious

   b. humorous

   c. silly

   d. sad

B. Consider the issues. Work with a partner to answer the questions below.

1. Do you think Lee Fong Gwo should be paid for his part on the song "Return to Innocence?" Why or why not?

2. In the interview, Professor Hsu Chang-Wei says, "It's really more a moral issue than a legal one." Do you agree with him? Why or why not?

3. Since this interview, Professor Hsu Chang-Wei has received a check for US$2000 from the band Enigma. He sent this money to an Ami community trust fund. Do you think this should end the debate? Why or why not?

Reading Skill

Scanning
When you need to find specific information in a text, you should scan it, or move your eyes very quickly across the text without reading every word, stopping only to "pick up" the information you are looking for.

A. Scan the text on pages 48–50 to find the specific information below. Remember to look quickly over the text without reading every word.

1. How old was Lee Fong Gwo at the time of this interview?

   _____

2. In what year did the Ami singers travel to Europe?

   _____

3. What is the name of the Director of the Taiwan Association of Copyright Owners? _____

4. When did Enigma record "Return to Innocence"?

   _____

5. When did Enigma first hear the Ami Song? _____

B. The Web page below is about the group Enigma. Scan it to find these things:

1. The number of press articles listed _____

2. The cost of *The Screen Behind the Mirror* CD in US dollars _____

3. The name of the Canadian website which sells the CD

   _____

4. The date of the recommended interview _____

THE ENIGMA ARCHIVES

presents a new CD from Enigma:

THE SCREEN BEHIND THE MIRROR

January 17, 2000 (US/Europe)
February 7, 2000 (Australia)

Where to Buy It (buying from links with an asterisk help support this website!)

Borders* (US$12.59) has it bundled with the a promo copy of the first single for free!
CD Now* and **Amazon.com*** both have it for US$12.59
HMV UK (£11.99) has it in limited edition Digipak packaging with more artwork
CD Plus Canada (CDN$14.99) has it in stock

Disclaimer: The Enigma Archives does not endorse, nor is responsible for purchasing from, any of the above sites.

Press Articles

Gravity of Love (Review) 21-Jan-2000
Spotlight: Gravity of Love (Review) 15-Jan-2000
Review: The Screen Behind the Mirror 08-Jan-2000
The Screen Behind the Mirror (Interview) Dec-1999 *RECOMMENDED*

Reviews & Previews

Track-by-track review by Martyn Woolley
Long review by Joar Grimstvedt
Track-by-track review by Steven de Jong

Building Vocabulary

Grouping words
Putting words in groups helps you learn and remember them.

A. The music-related words below are from the reading on pages 48–50. Group these words in the chart below. Words that may be either a noun or a verb will fit in more than one column.

singers	perform	sing	tape
chant	piece of music	composer	song
CD	recordings	a big hit	musicians
pop chart	pop group	concerts	record
band			

PEOPLE	THINGS	ACTIVITIES

B. Add three more music-related words to the chart above.

Present perfect

Form: *have / has* + past participle.

Meaning: The **present perfect** is used to refer to events or actions that happened at a time in the past that is not specific, or that began in the past and continue to the present.

Over the past decade, combining traditional music with jazz **has become** *commonplace.*
For thousands of years, Lee Fong Gwo's family **has made** *a living growing rice.*

A. Complete the sentences below with the present perfect form of the verbs in parentheses.

1. Lee Fong Gwo's family _____ (be) in Taiwan for thousands of years.

2. Over the years, the group Enigma _____ (make) a lot of money from its recordings.

3. Lee Fong Gwo _____ (travel) to Europe at least once.

4. Many people _____ (forget) what traditional musical instruments look like.

5. Since Lee Fong Gwo _____ (live) his whole life in the town of Taitung, he must know a lot of people there.

6. The French government _____ (not/respond) to the Ami leaders.

B. Simple past or present perfect? Underline the correct verb form in parentheses. **Hint:** *The simple past is used to refer to actions or events that began and ended at a specific time in the past.*

Example: Lee Fong Gwo (<u>learned</u> / has learned) to sing when he was a child.

1. When Lee Fong Gwo was a child, his family (sang / has sung) together while they worked in the fields.

2. Lee Fong Gwo (lived / has lived) in Taiwan for his whole life.

3. In 1992, the musicians of Enigma (purchased / have purchased) the rights to the music from the French government.

4. The song "Return to Innocence" (was / has been) on the pop charts for more than six months in 1994.

5. The world (lost / has lost) many examples of traditional music.

6. The Enigma musicians (responded / have responded) to the Ami people at least once so far, but the debate continues.

Discussion & Writing

1. According to the reading in this chapter, it has become commonplace to combine traditional music from Africa, Latin America, and Asia with pop and jazz. What examples of this "mixing" can you think of? Why do you think this type of music has become popular?

2. Introduce your classmates to a musician or group of musicians that you especially like. If possible, bring in a recording of the music and play an excerpt.

3. Follow the instructions below to play the game Twenty Questions.

   STEP 1 Form a team of six to eight people. Work as a team to choose a musician or music group that everyone knows. Then, spend several minutes sharing what you know about the musician or group.

   STEP 2 Now get together with another team to see if they can guess the name of the musician or music group that your group chose following the instructions below.

   Rules:
   - The opposing team can only ask questions that can be answered with *Yes* or *No*.

   - The opposing team may ask only 20 questions. If they can't guess the musician or group in 20 questions, your team wins.

   Sample questions: Is it a group?
   Are they popular now?
   Do they play reggae?
   Are they British?

Crossword Puzzle

Use words from the reading to complete the crossword puzzle.

Across:

1 Another word for *uncommon* is ___. (line 44)

2 Lee Fong Gwo makes a living as a rice ___.

4 The person who writes music is called a ___.

5 The past form of *lead* is ___.

6 The Ami ___ to Taiwan from the islands of Southeast Asia.

7 The past form of *sing* is ___.

12 The daughter of your son or daughter would be your ___.

14 The singular form of *were* is ___.

17 The verbs to *empty* and to ___ are opposite in meaning.

18 CDs and cassette tapes are types of ___.

19 A very successful record is called a big ___. (line 9)

20 Another word for *bought* is ___. (line 50)

Down:

1 The opposite of *forgets* is ___.

2 The past tense of *feel* is ___.

3 Am, is ___.

8 A father, his daughter, and her child represent three ___ of a family. (line 70)

9 The opposite of *youngest* is ___.

10 The opposite of *northern* is ___.

11 Another word for *entire* is ___. (line 20)

13 The past tense of *reply* is ___.

15 The past tense of *spend* is ___.

16 The past form of *sell* is ___.

Chapter Focus

CONTENT:
Preparing and making a
good speech

READING SKILL:
Paying attention to headings

*BUILDING
VOCABULARY:*
Using powerful verbs

LANGUAGE FOCUS:
Understanding imperatives

*"There are three
things to remember
when making a
speech: Be brief,
be brilliant, and
be gone."*

— *Joke told by American
businesspeople before
giving a speech*

Chapter 6 How to Make a Speech

Before You Read

1. The woman on the facing page is making a speech. Have you ever made a speech? What was the topic? Whom did you speak to?

2. What are the most important parts of a good speech? With a partner, rank the following from most important (1) to least important (5). Explain your choices to another pair.

   _____ Choosing an interesting topic

   _____ Telling jokes and funny stories

   _____ Making eye contact

   _____ Teaching the audience something new

   _____ Keeping the speech short

3. George Plimpton, the author of "How to Make a Speech," is a famous writer and speechmaker. In the article on pages 60–62, he gives some suggestions on how to make a good speech. As you read, write down three of his suggestions.

HOW TO MAKE A SPEECH

by George Plimpton

from *How to Use the Power of the Printed Word*

1　One of life's terrors for the uninitiated[1] is to be asked to make a speech.

"Why me?" will probably be your first reaction. "I don't have anything to say." The fact is that each one of us has a store of material which should be of interest to others. There is no reason why it should not
5　be adapted to a speech.

Why Know How to Speak?

Scary as it is, it's important for anyone to be able to speak in front of others, whether twenty around a conference table or a hall filled with a thousand faces.

10　Being able to speak can mean better grades in any class. It can mean talking the **town council** out of increasing your **property taxes**. It can mean talking top management into buying your plan.

How to Pick a Topic

You were probably asked to speak in the first place in the hope that
15　you would be able to articulate a topic that you know something about. Still, it helps to find out about your audience first. Who are they? Why are they there? What are they interested in? How much do you already know about your subject?

How to Plan What to Say

20　Here is where you must do your homework.

The more you sweat in advance, the less you'll have to sweat once you appear on stage. Research your topic thoroughly. Check the library for facts, quotes, books, and timely magazine and newspaper articles on your subject. Get in touch with experts. Write to them,
25　make phone calls, get interviews to help round out your material.[2] In short, gather—and learn—far more than you'll ever use. You can't imagine how much confidence that knowledge will inspire.

Now start organizing and writing. Most authorities suggest that a good speech breaks down into three basic parts: an introduction, the
30　body of the speech, and the summation.

---

[1] **the uninitiated**　people doing something for the first time

[2] **round out your material**　complete your research

- *Introduction*: An audience makes up its mind very quickly. Once the mood of an audience is set, it is difficult to change it, which is why introductions are important. If the speech is to be lighthearted in tone,[3] the speaker can start off by telling a good-natured story[4] about
35 the subject or himself.

- *Main body*: There are four main intents[5] in the body of the well-made speech. These are (1) to entertain, which is probably the hardest; (2) to instruct, which is the easiest if the speaker has done the research and knows the subject; (3) to persuade, which one does
40 at a sales presentation, a **political rally**, or a town meeting; and finally, (4) to inspire, which is what the speaker emphasizes at a sales meeting, in a sermon, or at a pep rally.

- *Summation*: An ending should probably incorporate a sentence or two which sounds like an ending—a short summary of the main
45 points of the speech, perhaps, or the repeat of a phrase that most embodies what the speaker has hoped to convey. It is valuable to think of the last sentence or two as something which might produce applause. Phrases which are perfectly appropriate to signal this are: "In closing. . ." or "I have one last thing to say. . ."

50 **How to Sound Spontaneous**

The best speakers are those who make their words sound spontaneous even if memorized. I've found it's best to learn a speech point by point, not word for word. Careful preparation and a great deal of practicing are required to make it come together smoothly
55 and easily. **Mark Twain** once said, "It takes three weeks to prepare a good ad-lib speech.[6]"

Brevity Is an Asset[8]

A sensible plan, if you have been asked to speak to an exact limit, is to talk your speech into a mirror and stop at your allotted time;[7] then
60 cut the speech accordingly. The more familiar you become with your speech, the more confidently you can deliver it.

As anyone who listens to speeches knows, brevity is an asset. Twenty minutes are ideal. An hour is the limit an audience can listen comfortably.

---

[3] **lighthearted in tone**   amusing; not serious

[4] **good-natured story**   funny story

[5] **intents**   purposes

[6] **ad-lib speech**   public talk that is not carefully prepared in advance

[7] **allotted time**   maximum amount of time given

[8] **brevity is an asset**   shortness is a good thing

65 How Questions Help

A question period at the end of a speech is a good notion. One would not ask questions following a **tribute to the company treasurer on his retirement**, say, but a technical talk or an informative speech can be enlivened with a question period.

70 The Crowd

The larger the crowd, the easier it is to speak, because the response is multiplied and increased. Most people do not believe this. They peek out[9] from behind the curtain, and if the audience is filled to the rafters,[10] they begin to moan softly in the back of their throats.

75 What About Stage Fright?

Very few speakers escape the so-called "butterflies.[11]" There does not seem to be any cure for them, except to realize that they are beneficial rather than harmful, and never fatal. The tension usually means that the speaker, being keyed up,[12] will do a better job.

80 **Edward R. Murrow** called stage fright "the sweat of perfection." Mark Twain once comforted a fright-frozen[13] friend about to speak: "Just remember they don't expect much." My own feeling is that with thought, preparation, and faith in your ideas, you can go out there and expect a pleasant surprise.

About the | Author

George Plimpton (1927–2003) was a writer, public speaker, editor, and actor who lived in New York. He is best known for participating in many of the activities he wrote about. He trained with a professional football team, boxed three rounds with a light-heavyweight champion, and played on the professional golf circuit.

---

9 **peek out**   look out timidly
10 **filled to the rafters**   full of people
11 **the so-called "butterflies"**   nervous feelings in one's stomach
12 **keyed up**   excited and nervous
13 **fright-frozen**   very nervous or scared

After You Read

Understanding the Text

A. Multiple choice. For each item below, circle the best answer.

1. The main idea of the reading is:

   a. It's very difficult to give a good speech.

   b. With a lot of research and practice, anyone can learn how to give a good speech.

   c. The three basic parts of a speech are the introduction, the main body, and the summation.

   d. Choosing a good topic is the most important part of making a good speech.

2. When preparing to make a speech, the first thing a speaker should do is:

   a. choose a topic

   b. understand who the audience will be

   c. do a lot of research on the topic

   d. organize the speech

3. According to the author, which of the following is the most difficult to accomplish in giving a speech:

   a. instruct

   b. inspire

   c. entertain

   d. persuade

4. The ideal length for a speech is:

   a. as short as possible

   b. 20 minutes long

   c. 20–60 minutes long

   d. It depends on the topic.

5. The overall tone of the reading is:

   a. serious and academic

   b. light and silly

   c. informative and humorous

   d. scientific and technical

B. Consider the issues. Work with a partner to answer the questions below.

1. What are the best ways to research a topic before writing a speech?

2. Everyone gets nervous before giving a speech. What can a speaker do to feel more relaxed and confident?

3. What are some things a person can do to sound spontaneous? Why is it important to sound spontaneous when giving a speech?

Reading Skill

Paying attention to headings
A **heading** is a small group of words that serves as a title for a paragraph or several paragraphs:

How to Pick a Topic

You were probably asked to speak in the first place in the hope that you would be able to articulate a topic that you know something about. Still, it helps to find out . . .

When a reading is long or complicated, authors use headings to help guide the reader. Headings divide a reading into smaller parts and help the reader find specific information quickly.

Look back at the reading to answer the questions below:

1. How many headings does the author use? _____

2. Under which heading does the author talk about doing research?

   _____

3. Under which heading can you find information on the ideal length for a

   speech? _____

   _____

4. Why do you think the author chose to use so many headings for this

   article? _____

   _____

Using powerful verbs
Some verbs like *lead*, *manage*, or *inspire* are strong and forceful. They demonstrate action and authority. These verbs create an impression of confidence when you are writing résumés, letters of application, or other business documents.

A. For each item below, two of the three words are similar in meaning to the **boldface** word. Cross out the word that is <u>not</u> similar in meaning to the other three. Use your dictionary or thesaurus if you need help.

1. **persuade**	**a.** convince	**b.** talk into	**c.** ~~deny~~
2. **articulate**	**a.** talk about	**b.** reject	**c.** express
3. **inspire**	**a.** excite	**b.** motivate	**c.** bore
4. **emphasize**	**a.** minimize	**b.** stress	**c.** highlight
5. **incorporate**	**a.** include	**b.** integrate	**c.** forget
6. **convey**	**a.** communicate	**b.** excite	**c.** transmit
7. **enliven**	**a.** jazz up	**b.** stimulate	**c.** satisfy
8. **instruct**	**a.** give	**b.** teach	**c.** educate

B. Complete each sentence with the past tense form of one of the boldface words in **A**. More than one answer is possible.

1. Ann _____ her husband to stop smoking by showing him many reports on the dangers of tobacco.

2. The car manufacturer _____ several new safety features into this year's model.

3. With his charisma, energy, and ideas, John F. Kennedy _____ Americans to accomplish great things like putting a man on the moon.

4. The Japanese professor _____ his students in the language and culture of Japan.

5. The band _____ the wedding reception with loud and fast-paced music for the guests to dance to.

6. The President _____ his three-point health care plan by carefully outlining each point in great detail.

7. The treasurer _____ the need to control expenses by mentioning five times that all employees must carefully monitor their spending.

8. At William's funeral, his friends _____ their sympathy to William's wife.

Language Focus

Understanding imperatives

We often use **imperatives** when making commands. For example: *Wake up! Don't be late!* We also use imperatives to:

- Make requests — *Please close the window.*
- Give advice — *Don't forget Father's Day.*
- Give directions — *Take a right on Maple Street.*
- Give warnings — *Watch out!*
- Explain procedures — *Mix two cups of sugar with one cup of flour.*

When we use an imperative, the subject of the sentence is always understood to be you (singular or plural).

Reread lines 21–27 of the reading, and then answer the questions below.

1. Write down all of the *imperatives* the author uses in this paragraph.

_____

_____

2. What is his purpose in using these imperatives (e.g., to give a warning)?

_____

_____

1. You are going to give a speech to your classmates. Choose one of the topics below and put a check (√) beside it. If you have your own idea, write it on the line.

   ☐ how to form a study group
   ☐ how to ask your boss for a raise
   ☐ how to make guests feel comfortable at a party
   ☐ how to ask someone out on a date
   ☐ how to (your own idea) _____

2. Now think of 4–5 important points about your topic that you would like to include in your speech and write them below.

IMPORTANT POINTS

3. Prepare a five-minute speech on your topic. Use this presentation outline to help you.

INTRODUCTION

"My name is ____ and I am delighted to be here today. I'd like to speak to you about . . ."

ORGANIZATION

"I have divided my talk into three parts . . ."

MAIN PARTS

"First . . ."

"That brings me to . . ."

"Finally . . ."

CONCLUSION

"In closing . . ."

Crossword Puzzle

Use words from the reading to complete the crossword puzzle.

Across:

2 The opposite of the *beginning* is the ___.

4 The main or central part of a speech is called the ___.

6 The noun form of the verb *prepare* is ___.

9 take, took, ___

10 Another word for *frightening* is ___. (line 7)

11 The ideal length of time for a speech is ___ minutes.

14 The more you do now, the ___ you will have to do later.

15 The three basic parts of a good speech are the introduction, the body, and the ___.

16 The opposite of *decreasing* is ___.

Down:

1 Another word for *teach* is ___. (line 38)

3 An expert is someone who is an ___ on a particular topic. (line 28)

4 The opposite of *harmful* is ___. (line 78)

5 A speaker gives, or ___, a speech. (line 61)

7 Another word for choose is ___.

8 There are four main goals of a good speech. The most difficult is to ___. (line 37)

12 *Z* is the ___ letter in the English alphabet.

13 A synonym for *wish* is ___.

Chapter Focus

CONTENT:
Having a special place to go
to reflect on life

READING SKILL:
Supporting main ideas

**BUILDING
VOCABULARY:**
Using context to guess
meaning

LANGUAGE FOCUS:
Talking about the past

"Solitude is good company."

— *Luis Barragan*
Mexican architect
(1902 – 1988)

Chapter ▲ 7 Private Lives

Before You Read

1. The writer of this personal essay goes to the beach on a regular basis to think about her life. Why do you think she chose the beach as a good place for quiet reflection?

2. This personal essay is set in St. Petersburg, Florida. Look at the map on page 192. What can you learn about Florida from this information? Share your ideas with a partner.

3. Read the title of the essay on pages 72–73 and then take one minute to skim it. What do you think the essay will be about? Why?

PRIVATE LIVES

by Diane Daniel

from *The St. Petersburg Times*

Life seems a little less fragile[1] when you can depend on a special place to always be there for you.

1 There is a tiny slice of the **Gulf of Mexico** that belongs to me. Looking across the water, or down the shoreline, I see the past 20 years play over and over,[2] like an old **Super 8 movie**.

I'm 16, writing poetry while sitting on a bench at sunset. I'm
5 floating atop the salty sea on my yellow raft. I'm sitting at the water's edge, gathering a rainbow of shells. I'm in college, burgundy hair glistening.[3] I'm a working woman, thinking about my career, paying the bills. I'm heavy, I'm thin. My hair is long, short, long again. I'm happy, sad. Growing older, growing up.

10 My parents and I moved from **North Carolina** to St. Petersburg, **Florida**, when I was just about to start my senior year of high school. It was a difficult time to be uprooted; I had lived in North Carolina all my life. But I loved the water, so Florida seemed an okay place to live. I can't remember how I first chose my special beach at the end of
15 Eighth Avenue. But once I chose my spot, I never switched beaches.

Almost daily, I swam and sunned there. I watched the sun set. I thought about life. On weekend nights in college, I hung out[4] at the beach with friends, playing music or just listening to the waves. My bedroom at my parents' house holds no memories for me. My
20 memories of Florida are all a mile away, at Eighth Avenue beach.

I live in Boston now and visit my parents in Florida twice a year. Whenever I visit, I spend many hours at my beach, usually under a hot sun, but sometimes at night, when the sand is cool and the sea seems to offer answers it won't share during the day. I go to my beach not
25 only to relax and think, but also to feed off the sea.[5] The waves are

---

[1] **fragile**   easily hurt or broken

[2] **play over and over**   repeat themselves many times

[3] **burgundy hair glistening**   red hair shining

[4] **hung out**   relaxed

[5] **feed off the sea**   get energy and inspiration from the ocean

gentle, the water soothing. But more important to me is the sea's permanence and sheer force.[6] I want to be strong like that.

30   During one visit to Florida last year, I was sad about the end of a relationship, and I knew that my sadness would worry my parents. I had to stop at Eighth Avenue before I could see them. After flying in from Boston, I drove straight to the beach. It was late afternoon in May, and the sun had softened. When I reached the beach, I parked at the end of Eighth Avenue and slowly walked barefoot to the water. I tasted the gulf, and with it, some hope.

35   I have taken a few friends to my sanctuary,[7] but it's not a place I share with many. Five years ago I brought Jack, a former **boyfriend,** and I'm glad I did. Now when I look down the shore or across the water, he is there, too, laughing at the pelicans as they dive for food, holding me while we watch the sunset from the edge of the water.

40   Jack will always be there. So will my friend JoEllen, who came to Eighth Avenue with me a couple of years ago. We walked and walked until the sun and sand had exhausted us. Sometimes I talk my mother into[8] going to watch the sunset, and we sit on the bench, appreciating our time together.

45   Last year, I had planned to take Tom to Eighth Avenue. He was going to be the most important visitor of all, the person I thought I would spend the rest of my life with. A few days before we were supposed to leave, he changed his mind, about the trip to Florida and about us. I'm glad he never saw my beach.

50   As long as my parents are alive, I will go to Eighth Avenue. It has occurred to me that I will probably mourn their deaths there, listening to the waves and watching the gulls. I wonder how often I will see my beach after my parents are gone. I'm sure I will go there from time to time, maybe even stay in one of the cottages nearby that
55   I've passed so often. But it doesn't matter. My tiny slice of the Gulf of Mexico is always within reach.

About the Author

Diane Daniel (1957–) is a journalist at *The Boston Globe*, a major daily newspaper for the Boston area. She writes personal essays as well as articles about travel, the arts, and home design.

---

[6] **sheer force**   great strength

[7] **sanctuary**   safe, protected place

[8] **talk my mother into**   convince my mother to

After You Read

Understanding the Text

A. Multiple choice. For each item below, circle the best answer:

1. The main idea of the reading is:
   a. You should only bring a few close friends to your special place.
   b. The Eighth Avenue beach has played an important role in the author's life for the past 20 years.
   c. You need to be alone to solve your problems.
   d. When you end a significant relationship, it's a good idea to spend time alone at your special place.

2. The author chose her special beach when she _____, and never changed beaches after that.
   a. started high school
   b. moved to North Carolina
   c. was in college
   d. moved to Florida

3. The author has already done all of the following at the Eighth Avenue beach except:
   a. play music and write poetry
   b. watch the sunset with a boyfriend
   c. mourn the death of a family member
   d. take long walks and collect shells

4. In line 40, the sentence "Jack will always be there" means:
   a. Jack lives near the Eighth Avenue beach.
   b. Jack accompanies the author to her special beach every time she goes.
   c. When the author visits or thinks about her beach, she remembers the time she spent there with Jack.
   d. Visiting the Eighth Avenue beach was the highlight of the author's relationship with Jack.

5. All of the following statements are probably true about the author except:

    a. She has positive feelings about Jack.

    b. She has always liked the ocean.

    c. She and Tom had talked about getting married.

    d. She has always been slim.

6. The overall tone of the reading is:

    a. personal and reflective

    b. serious and informative

    c. sad and depressing

    d. light and romantic

B. Consider the issues. Work with a partner to answer the questions below.

    1. Why does the author keep going back to the beach?

    2. What qualities of the sea are important for the author? Why?

    3. Why do you think the author is glad that Tom never saw her beach?

    4. Do you think the author feels happy or sad after visiting the beach?

Supporting main ideas
Writers usually focus on one or two **main ideas** in a piece of writing. They support their main ideas with details. These details help the reader understand and appreciate the writer's main ideas.

A. Look back at the reading and find at least three details that support the main idea given below.

MAIN IDEA
The Eighth Avenue beach has played an important role in the author's life for the past 20 years.
SUPPORTING DETAILS
1.
2.
3.

B. Look back at the reading in Chapter 2, Student Learning Teams, and find at least three details that support the main idea given below.

MAIN IDEA
Forming a learning team can improve your academic performance.
SUPPORTING DETAILS
1.
2.
3.

Using context to guess meaning

When you don't know the meaning of a word, look at the words around it to help you. You may be able to guess the meaning of the word from its surrounding context.

Complete the chart below with information about vocabulary in the reading. First guess the meaning, then give the reason for your guess.

Example: ...stay in one of the **cottages**... (line 54)

Meaning: *a cottage is a kind of house*

Reason: *We "stay" in houses.*

1. ...laughing at the **pelicans** as they dive for food... (line 38)

Meaning:

Reason:

2. ...walked **barefoot** to the water... (line 33)

Meaning:

Reason:

3. ...The waves are gentle, the water **soothing**... (line 26)

Meaning:

Reason:

4. ...floating atop the salty sea on my yellow **raft**... (line 5)

Meaning:

Reason:

5. ...**mourn** their deaths... (line 51)

Meaning:

Reason:

Talking about the past

We use the *simple past* to talk about an action or event that happened at a specific time in the past.
*My parents and I **moved** to Florida when I was 16.*

The *present perfect* is used to refer to an event or action that happened at a time in the past that is not specific, or that began in the past and continue to the present.
*I **have taken** a few friends to my sanctuary, but it's not a place I share with many.*

We use the *past perfect* to show that one event happened before another in the past.
*It was a difficult time to be uprooted; I **had lived** in North Carolina all my life.*

A. Find one or more additional examples of the simple past, present perfect, and past perfect to add to the chart below. Look back at the reading.

SIMPLE PAST	PRESENT PERFECT	PAST PERFECT
moved to Florida when I was 16	have taken a few friends to my sanctuary	had lived in North Carolina

B. Choose one example of the simple past, the present perfect and the past perfect from your list. Why did the author use the tense in each of these cases? Explain your ideas to a partner.

Example: It was a difficult time to be uprooted; **I had lived** in North Carolina all my life.

Reason: The author uses the past perfect to show that one action in the past happened before another. The author was born and lived in North Carolina and then, 16 years later, she moved to Florida.

1. The chart below lists several places where someone might go to reflect on life and gather strength. With a partner, give reasons why a person might choose each location as his or her special place.

LOCATIONS	REASONS
Beach	• likes the sound of waves
	• thinks swimming is relaxing
1. Top of a mountain	
2. Library	
3. Gym	
4. Church or temple	
5. Art museum	

2. What is the difference between being alone and being lonely? How does this quotation relate to ideas in the reading?

"Solitude is one thing and loneliness is another."
— *May Sarton, American poet (1912–1995)*

3. Do you have a special place where you go to reflect on life? Describe your special place. Tell how and when you chose your place, and why this particular place is important to you.

Use words from the reading to complete the crossword puzzle.

Across:

3 A ___ boyfriend is someone who used to be a boyfriend.

5 When you walk without your shoes on, you walk ___.

6 You can watch the sun ___ in the evening. (line 16)

7 The noun form of the adjective *sad* is ___.

9 Another word for *shining* is ___. (line 7)

11 A word for *very small* is ___.

14 If you drive ___ to a particular place, you go there directly. (line 31)

16 The opposite of *hate* is ___.

17 The past form of *choose* is ___.

18 The simple past of *drive* is ___.

Down:

1 The opposite of *rough* is ___. (line 26)

2 The simple past of the verb *swim* is ___.

4 The opposite of *weak* is ___.

7 Ocean water tastes ___ but most lake water does not.

8 The Earth moves around the ___.

10 Another word for *changed* is ___. (line 15)

12 ___ means *not at any time*.

13 One kilometer equals about six-tenths of a ___.

15 Two times a year is the same as ___ a year.

Bill Gates—Chairman of Microsoft Corporation

> *"My interest is in the future because I'm going to spend the rest of my life there."*
>
> — *Charles F. Kettering*
> *American scientist*
> *(1876 – 1958)*

Chapter Focus

CONTENT:
Communicating in the future

READING SKILL:
Using context

BUILDING VOCABULARY:
Word forms

LANGUAGE FOCUS:
too and enough

Chapter ▲ 8 Future Talk: A Conversation with Bill Gates

Before You Read

1. What are some of the ways you can communicate with people who are far away? How often do you use these means of communication?

2. Scan the interview on pages 84–86. Who is the person being interviewed? What do you already know about this person?

3. Group work. Discuss the questions in the chart below. Check (√) your group's answers in the chart.

QUESTIONS	ANSWERS
a. Will e-mail replace all regular mail in the future?	☐ YES ☐ NO
b. Will people use pens and pencils less in the future?	☐ YES ☐ NO
c. Will people who don't have computer skills be able to find work?	☐ YES ☐ NO
d. Will public telephones receive pictures as well as sound?	☐ YES ☐ NO
e. Will everyone be able to work on computers at home and never have to go to an office?	☐ YES ☐ NO

FUTURE TALK

A Conversation with **Bill Gates**
Chairman, Microsoft Corporation

—interviewed by Larry King of CNN

1   **LARRY KING:** I'm having this conversation with you on a computer, and I'm wondering if e-mail is going to replace the post office in the future.

BILL GATES: E-mail won't replace the post office, but it will replace
5   a lot of paper the post office and overnight services carry around today.

KING: Do you worry your child won't learn penmanship[1] because there's always a keyboard and a printer nearby?

GATES: When I was in school, I always felt it was unfair that kids who
10   happened to have bad handwriting were penalized at grade time.[2] Obviously, everybody needs to learn basic writing skills. We want our kids to have a full complement of[3] basic communications skills. I'm a lot more concerned that kids who only use calculators and never learn to do multiplication and division by hand may fail to grasp[4] the
15   basics of mathematics.

KING: Will there be any use for pencils and paper?

GATES: People will use pencils and paper for a long time but they won't use them as much as they do now.

KING: Tell me how a computer will be used in the average home thirty
20   years from now.

GATES: You'll have lots of thin flat screens covering walls of your house and you'll carry a hand-held device around with you. The screens will feed whatever visual information you want—live video from a place in the world you like, an art reproduction, or maybe a
25   **stock ticker.**

---

[1] **penmanship**   handwriting

[2] **were penalized at grade time**   were given a lower grade as punishment

[3] **full complement of**   a complete set of

[4] **may fail to grasp**   may not learn

KING: What happens when the power goes out?[5]

GATES: We're very dependent today on electricity and we still will be in fifty years. If there's a power failure, you won't get much work done, although battery technology will improve enough that short
30   power failures won't necessarily shut down[6] all of your computers.

KING: Are we going to get television and news and entertainment from the Internet rather than from a set hooked to cable in the house?

GATES: News and entertainment will be delivered from the Internet to cable television[7] and telephone connections in our homes. We'll
35   access this information[8] using a variety of devices, some of which will resemble[9] today's televisions.

KING: Will a person be able to work in the future without having any computer skills?

GATES: There will still be jobs for people without computer skills, but
40   a smaller percentage than exist today. The proportion of the workforce that lacks computer skills will decrease as people not having those skills get retrained or retire. Most young people have computer skills or at least an enthusiasm to get them.

KING: Describe an office in the future. Telephone? Fax machine?
45   Conference room? Will there be an office building?

GATES: The key element of the office of the future is that it will have lots of flat screens, just like your house will. And these screens are going to be everywhere once they get thin enough, cheap enough, and high enough in quality. You'll carry around a lightweight screen the
50   way you carry a wallet or cell phone or newspaper today.

The notion of[10] a fax will disappear because documents will be transferred electronically without having to pass through the intermediate stage of being printed on paper. If the recipient[11] wants to read it on paper, she'll print it.

---

[5] **when the power goes out**   when electric power fails or stops

[6] **shut down**   stop

[7] **cable television**   a television service that provides programs to paying customers

[8] **access this information**   get this information

[9] **resemble**   look like

[10] **the notion of**   the idea of

[11] **the recipient**   the receiver

55 "Telephone" refers to an audio-only electronic communications link, and we'll continue to have this kind of connection. But I think audio-only communication will be the exception rather than the rule.[12] Communications will usually involve **videoconferencing**, collaborative work on a document, or some other kind of data
60 interchange beyond audio alone. We'll have conference rooms, but some of the participants in a conference may be in other places and hooked in electronically. Some will participate from home when being face-to-face isn't important. Office buildings and even cities may lose some of their importance because the Internet and
65 corporate intranets[13] will enable workers to communicate, share information, store data, and collaborate regardless of where they are.

KING: What worries you about the future?

GATES: The world's rapidly growing population concerns me. We need to encourage people to start thinking about the consequences of
70 having too many people on the planet—food and water shortages, pollution, too many people crammed into drug-infested[14] and violence-filled urban centers.

About the Author

Larry King is the host of a popular late night television show, *Larry King Live*. This interview is from the book *Future Talk, Conversations about Tomorrow with Today's Most Provocative Personalities* by Larry King with Pat Piper. King is known for his intense interview style and high profile guests including politicians, actors, artists, scientists, and royalty.

---

[12] **be the exception rather than the rule**   be uncommon or infrequent

[13] **corporate intranets**   internet-type networks linking employees within a company

[14] **drug-infested**   filled with drugs

After You Read

Understanding the Text

A. **True or False?** Read the statements below and write T (True) or F (False).

_____ 1. Gates believes that soon we won't be dependent on electricity.

_____ 2. According to Gates, it will be possible to participate in office meetings and conferences from your home.

_____ 3. In Gates' opinion, it will become more common to get visual information on computers.

_____ 4. Gates thinks we'll use more paper in the future.

_____ 5. According to Gates, audio-only communication will be the most popular way to communicate with people far away.

_____ 6. You can infer that Gates believes people will continue to write by hand.

B. **Consider the Issues.** Work with a partner to answer the questions below.

1. Check (√) if you agree or disagree with each of Gates' opinions in the chart below. Then explain why.

a. In the future, there will still be some jobs for people without computer skills.

☐ Agree Why? _____

☐ Disagree _____

b. Children will still need to have basic communication skills.

☐ Agree Why? _____

☐ Disagree _____

c. The world's population is a serious problem.

☐ Agree Why? _____

☐ Disagree _____

2. The interview on pages 84–86 was conducted by e-mail. Which statements below describe an e-mail interview? Check (√) them.

_____ **a.** You don't have to be in the same place for the interview.

_____ **b.** You can do some research before answering a question.

_____ **c.** You can see how the person is reacting to your questions.

_____ **d.** You can interrupt the other person.

_____ **e.** You can think for a long time before you answer a question.

_____ **f.** You have to dress up.

_____ **g.** The interview can take place over a period of days.

3. Would you rather be interviewed by e-mail or in person? Why?

Reading Skill

Using context

Many words have more than one meaning. That's why it's important to use **context** (the surrounding words and ideas) to make sure you understand a word.

Read each sentence below and use context to guess the meaning of the italicized word. Then underline the best definition from the dictionary entry or entries.

1. I'm a lot more concerned that kids who only use calculators may fail to *grasp* the basics of mathematics.

> **grasp** /graːsp/ *verb* **1** to take hold of somebody/something suddenly and firmly: *Lisa grasped the child firmly by the hand.* (figurative) to grasp an opportunity **2** to understand something: *I don't think you've grasped how serious this is.*

2. The screens will *feed* whatever visual information you want—live video from a place in the world you like, an art reproduction, or maybe a stock ticker.

> **feed** /fiːd/ *verb* **1** to give food to a person or an animal: *Don't forget to feed the dog. I can't come yet. I haven't fed the baby.* **2** (used about animals) to eat: *What do horses feed on in the winter?* **3** to provide advice, information, especially regularly: *Computers feed news reports on an hourly basis.*

3. Are we going to get television and news and entertainment from the Internet rather than from a set *hooked* up to cable in the house?

> **hook** /hʊk/ *verb* **1** to fasten something or to be fastened with a hook or something like a hook **2** to catch hold of something with a hook or with something shaped like a hook
>
> **be/get hooked (on something)** *(slang)* **1** to like (doing) something very much: *Brian is hooked on computer games.* **2** to be unable to stop using drugs, alcohol, etc.: *to be hooked on gambling*
>
> **hook something up (to something)** to connect a machine, etc. to a larger system so that it can work: *You can't call me at my new apartment—the phone isn't hooked up yet.*

4. We need to encourage people to start thinking about the consequences of having too many people *crammed* into drug-infested and violence-filled urban centers.

> **cram** /kræm/ *verb* (cramming; crammed) **1** to push people or things into a small space: *I managed to cram all my clothes into the bag, but I couldn't zip it up. We only spent two days in New York, but we crammed in a lot of sightseeing.* **2** to move, with a lot of other people, into a small space: *He only had a small car, but we all crammed into it.* **3** to study very hard and learn a lot in a short time before an examination: *She's cramming for her final exams.*

Building Vocabulary

A. Complete the chart below by adding the missing word forms. Then check your ideas by looking in a dictionary.

NOUN	VERB	ADJECTIVE
1. information		
2. entertainment		
3. variety		
4. communication		
5.	resemble	X
6.	collaborate	

B. Choose words from the chart in **A** to complete these sentences. More than one answer may be possible.

1. Do you think the interview with Bill Gates was very _____?

2. What forms of _____ can you get from the Internet?

3. Larry King asked Bill Gates a _____ of questions dealing with the topic of communications.

4. It is difficult to interview someone who is not very _____.

5. Is there any _____ between the first television and today's television?

6. Many people _____ in the development of the Internet.

Too* and *enough

We use *too* to describe an excessive amount of something.
We use *enough* to describe a sufficient amount.
We use *not + enough* to describe an insufficient amount.

- *Don't watch too much TV.*
- *These screens are going to be everywhere once they get thin* **enough**, *cheap* **enough**, *and high* **enough** *in quality.*
- *Battery technology will improve* **enough** *that short power failures won't shut down all computers.*
- *Many people worry that there will* **not** *be* **enough** *food and water for everyone on the planet.*

What is there too much of in the world today? What is there not enough of? Put each word in the box under one of the sentences below. Then add more words of your own.

cars	happiness	doctors	people
food	fighting	violence	pollution

1. There is too much _____ in the world today.	**2. There are too many _____ in the world today.**	**3. There isn't/ aren't enough _____ in the world today.**
_____	_____	_____
_____	_____	_____
_____	_____	_____

A. Bill Gates says that rapid population growth worries him. What problems worry you about the future? Why? Discuss your ideas with a partner.

B. Follow the suggestions below to get your classmates' opinions about the future.

1. Work in groups to come up with four questions about the future, beginning with the question starters below. Write your questions on another piece of paper.

Question Starters	Examples
Will there be any use for . . .	Will there be any use for *pencils and paper?* Will there be any use for *libraries?*
Do you worry. . .	Do you worry *your children won't learn penmanship?* Do you worry *people will live too long?*
Will a person be able to . . .	Will a person be able to *work without having any computer skills?* Will a person be able to *live for 300 years?*
Describe . . .	Describe *an office in the future.* Describe *a kitchen in the future.*

2. Exchange your list of questions with another group. As a group discuss and answer the questions you received and write down your answers.

3. Share your answers with the rest of the class by reading the questions you got and the answers your group came up with.

Crossword Puzzle

Use words from the reading to complete the crossword puzzle.

Across:

5 Another word for a *meeting* room is a ___ room. (line 45)

6 Waitressing, selling clothes, and repairing cars are types of ___.

8 Another word for *handwriting* is ___. (line 7)

10 Another word for *connected* is ___. (line 32)

13 A person who *participates* is a ___.

14 A tabletop is ___, a ball is not. (line 21)

15 The opposite of *success* is ___. (line 28)

16 ___ means *low in price*.

17 Another word for *connections* is ___. (line 55)

Down:

1 The future is any time after ___.

2 When you type information into a computer, you use a ___.

3 The opposite of *off* is ___.

4 I, ___; we, us

7 The opposite of *thick* is ___.

9 If there is not enough water, you can say there is a water ___. (line 70)

11 The opposite of *increase* is ___.

12 An opposite of *slowly* is ___. (line 68)

15 The past tense of *feel* is ___.

18 The opposite of *yes* is ___.

> ## "Every man's work, whether it be literature or music or pictures or architecture or anything else, is always a portrait of himself."

— *Samuel Butler*
English writer
(1835 – 1902)

Chapter Focus

CONTENT:
Applying for a job

READING SKILL:
Reading instructional materials

BUILDING VOCABULARY:
Using connecting words

LANGUAGE FOCUS:
Giving advice

Chapter ▲ 9 Letters of Application

Before You Read

1. Have you ever had a full or part-time job? How did you get your job? Share your experiences with a partner.

2. Read the title of the article on pages 96–98 and then take one minute to skim it. What do you think the article will be about? Share your ideas with a partner.

3. In the chart below, check (√) *True* or *False* for each of the statements. Then, read the article to confirm your guesses.

STATEMENT	TRUE	FALSE
a. The reason for writing a letter of application is to get a job interview.	☐	☐
b. When sending a letter of application you must always send a résumé[1], too.	☐	☐
c. It's a good idea to talk about your best qualities and biggest accomplishments in a letter of application.	☐	☐
d. You should mention the salary you want in a letter of application.	☐	☐

---

[1] **résumé**   one or two-page summary of your education and work experience

LETTERS OF APPLICATION

by Andrea B. Geffner

from *Business Letters the Easy Way*

1   A **letter of application** is a sales letter in which you are both salesperson and product, for the purpose of an application is to attract an employer's attention and persuade him or her to grant you an interview.[2] To do this, the letter presents what you can offer the
5   employer, rather than what you want from the job.

   Like a **résumé**, the letter of application is a sample of your work; and it is, as well, an opportunity to demonstrate, not just talk about, your skills and personality. If it is written with flair[3] and understanding and prepared with professional care, it is likely to hit
10   its mark.[4]

   There are two types of application letters. A *solicited* letter (see page 106) is sent in response to a **help-wanted ad.** Because such a letter will be in competition with many, perhaps several hundred others, it must be composed with distinction.[5] At the same time, it
15   must refer to the ad and the specific job advertised.

   An *unsolicited* letter is sent to a company for which you would like to work though you know of no particular opening. The advantage of this type of application, however, is that there will be little competition and you can define yourself the position you would like to apply for.
20   You can send out as many letters as you wish, to as many companies as you are aware of; it is a good idea, though, to find out the name of a specific person to whom you can send the letter—a more effective approach than simply addressing a letter to "**Personnel**."

   Because a letter of application must sell your qualifications,[6] it
25   must do more than simply restate your résumé in paragraph form.

---

[2] **grant you an interview**   schedule an interview with you

[3] **written with flair**   written with special skill and style

[4] **hit the mark**   be very effective

[5] **composed with distinction**   written extremely well

[6] **sell your qualifications**   present your skills and abilities in the best way

While the résumé must be factual, objective, and brief, the letter is your chance to interpret and expand. It should state explicitly how your background relates to the specific job, and it should emphasize your strongest and most pertinent characteristics.[7] The letter should
30   demonstrate that you know both yourself and the company.

A letter of application must communicate your ambition and enthusiasm. Yet it must, at the same time, be modest. It should be neither aggressive nor meek: neither pat yourself on the back[8] nor ask for sympathy. It should never express dissatisfaction with a
35   present or former job or employer. And you should avoid discussing your reasons for leaving your last job.

Keep in mind the following principles when writing your letter of application:

1. *Start by attracting attention.* You must say, of course, that you
40   are applying and mention both the specific job and how you heard about it. But try to avoid a mundane opening.[9] Instead of:

> *I would like to apply for the position of legal secretary which you advertised in the* Los Angeles Times *of Sunday, August 10 . . .*

45   **Try something a bit more original:**

> *I believe you will find my experiences in the Alameda* **District Attorney's** *office have prepared me well for the position of legal secretary which you advertised in the* Los Angeles Times *of Sunday, August 10 . . .*

50   **2.** *Continue by describing your qualifications.* Highlight your strengths and achievements and say how they suit you for the job at hand.[10] Provide details and explanations not found on your résumé, and refer the reader to the résumé for the remaining, less pertinent facts.

---

[7] **most pertinent characteristics**   qualities that are directly related to the job

[8] **pat yourself on the back**   give yourself credit for your accomplishments

[9] **mundane opening**   boring or unoriginal introduction

[10] **the job at hand**   the work to be done

55 **3.** *Assure the employer that you are the person for the job.* List verifiable facts[11] that prove you are not exaggerating or lying. Mention the names of any familiar or prominent **references** you may have. In some way, distinguish yourself from the mass of other qualified applicants.[12]

60 **4.** *Conclude by requesting an interview.* Urge the employer to action by making it easy to contact you. Mention your telephone number and the best hours to reach you, or state that you will call him or her within a few days.

A complete application should contain both a letter of application and a résumé. While it is possible to write a letter so complete in detail that a résumé seems redundant,[13] it is always most professional to include both.

Finally, a word about salary: basically, unless instructed by the want ad, it is best that you not broach the subject.[14] Indeed, even if an ad requires that you mention your salary requirements, it is advisable simply to call them "negotiable.[15]" However, when you go on an interview, you should be prepared to mention a salary range (e.g., $40,000 – $45,000). For this reason, you should investigate both your field and, if possible, the particular company. You don't want to ask for less than you deserve or more than is reasonable.

About the Author

Andrea B. Geffner is a business educator and writer. She is the former dean of the Taylor Business Institute in New York.

---

[11] **verifiable facts**   professional information that someone can easily check

[12] **mass of other qualified applicants**   all of the other qualified people who applied for the job

[13] **redundant**   unnecessary because it repeats the same information

[14] **broach the subject**   introduce the subject

[15] **negotiable**   something that can be changed after discussion

After You Read

Understanding the Text

A. Multiple choice. For each item below, circle the best answer.

1. The main purpose of this reading is to _____.

   a. show people how to write effective letters of application

   b. help people find interesting jobs

   c. explain the differences between a résumé and a letter of application

2. A letter written in response to a help-wanted ad is _____ letter.

   a. an unsolicited

   b. a solicited

   c. a reference

3. A letter of application should _____ the information contained in a résumé.

   a. restate

   b. not address

   c. expand upon

4. It is _____ to mention salary requirements in a letter of application.

   a. wise

   b. unnecessary

   c. inadvisable

5. The tone of a letter of application should be _____.

   a. polite and businesslike

   b. strong and aggressive

   c. friendly and personal

6. The author of this reading would probably agree that _____.

   a. résumés are more important than letters of application

   b. anyone can learn to write a good letter of application

   c. it is better to be too modest in a letter of application than too aggressive

B. Consider the issues. Work with a partner to answer the questions below.

1. According to the author, what are the things you *should* and *shouldn't* do when writing a letter of application? Group the eight ideas below into the correct columns in the chart. Then, try to add two ideas of your own to each column.

- *be original*
- *mention money*
- *give references*
- *sell yourself*
- *talk about good and bad former jobs*
- *make sure your letter stands out*
- *explain why you left your last job*
- *pat yourself on the back*

SHOULD	SHOULDN'T
be original	

2. It's a good idea to know some basic information about a company before you write a letter of application. What are three ways you can gather information on a new company before writing your letter?

3. Why is it important *not* to express dissatisfaction with a former job or employer in a letter of application or on an interview?

Reading instructional materials

Instructional materials tell you how to do something specific like study for an exam, fix your car, or take care of a baby. These readings often outline steps in a process or offer answers to specific questions people have. When you read instructional materials, think of specific questions you'd like to find answers for. It's not advisable to read instructional materials from beginning to end like a short story. Instead, scan these readings to quickly find the information you need.

The reading below is about going on a job interview. Scan the reading quickly to find the answers to the three questions below. Discuss your answers with a partner.

1. When you go on a job interview, what should you bring with you?

2. What important question should you ask before the end of an interview?

3. How should you end your follow-up letter?

BEFORE, DURING, AND AFTER A JOB INTERVIEW

by Peggy Schmidt

— from *The 90 Minute Interview Prep Book*

This section provides some guidelines that will help you have a good job interview.

Before the Interview

- Find out exactly who you will be interviewing with, including the person's name (ask for correct spelling) and title.

- Unless you know exactly where the interview location is, get directions. If you've never gone from your home to the interview location, go there at least once to familiarize yourself with the route and traffic conditions. On the day of the interview, allow extra time to get to your destination. It's far better to be early than late.

- Bring something to read while you wait in the reception area. A book or magazine is fine, but realize that the receptionist or the interviewer is likely to notice what you're reading. It's possible that the first question the interviewer may ask is, "How do you like the book?"

- Make sure your hands are clean and dry. Take time to wash your hands in the rest room before you meet the interviewer.

- Find out how much time the interviewer has. All you need to say is, "I know time is important to you. Could you let me know how much time we have?"

Before You Leave the Interview

- Thank the interviewer for the opportunity to meet with him or her. Mention your interest in the job and the company.

- Ask about the company's time frame for making a hiring decision.

- Ask if it's all right for you to call back in a week's time to check where things stand.[16]

Interview Follow-up

Writing a note to the person or people with whom you interviewed is an incredibly simple but important idea. And it can make the difference in getting hired.

1. Type the letter; it's more professional looking.

2. Thank the interviewer for talking to you. Mention something he or she said that was particularly interesting to you.

3. Explain in a sentence or two why you think you are a good match for the job or company. Be specific about what you think you can do for the company.

4. Conclude your letter by saying you hope to get the job and that you are happy to answer any additional questions that the interviewer has for you.

---

[16] **check where things stand**   see if the company has made a decision to hire anyone

Using connecting words

We use **connecting words** to show different kinds of relationships between phrases or sentences. These connecting words have different purposes including: adding new information, comparing and contrasting, showing a result, or emphasizing a point.

PURPOSE	CONNECTING WORDS	EXAMPLE FROM THE READING
Add new information	Also And In addition to	**In addition to** my administrative duties, I was responsible for scheduling all of Ms. Jenkins' appointments.
Compare and contrast	But Yet However	A letter of application must communicate your ambition and enthusiasm. **Yet**, it must, at the same time, be modest.
Show a result	Therefore Thus	Essentially, I did everything I could to make Ms. Jenkins' heavy responsibilities easier. **Thus**, I am familiar with the duties of an executive assistant and believe I am prepared to anticipate and meet all your expectations.
Emphasize a point	As a matter of fact Indeed	**Indeed**, even if an ad requires that you mention your salary requirements, it is advisable simply to call them "negotiable."

Read the story. Then write an appropriate connecting word from the box in the blanks below. More than one answer may be correct.

Therefore	In addition to	Yet
However	As a matter of fact	Thus

John's Interview

Soon after college graduation, John began to look for a job in the newspaper. John was excited when AJD Computers Inc. responded to his letter of application and asked him to come in for an interview. Because John hadn't gone on many interviews before, he was

nervous. (1)_____, he began to feel confident after he read *The 90-Minute Interview Prep Book.*

A few days before the interview, John took some steps to get ready. John knew he couldn't wear his usual casual jeans and

T-shirts. (2)_____ he went out and bought a suit.

(3)_____ calling for directions to the company, John familiarized himself with the route so he wouldn't get lost.

On the day of the interview, looking very professional in his new suit, John made sure to arrive at the interview early.

(4)_____, he was able to make a good first impression. The interviewer, Mr. Huber, was dressed very formally and it was obvious that he was a very important person in the

company. (5)_____ he had a warm and friendly smile that put John at ease.

Mr. Huber was so impressed with John's skills, experience, and attitude that he wanted to hire him right away.

(6)_____, he asked John to start the very next day. In the end, John accepted the position at a higher salary than he had hoped for.

Giving Advice

We use *should*, *must*, the imperative voice, and several different expressions to give advice.

Should:
*When you go on a job interview, you **should** be prepared to mention a salary range.*

Must:
*A letter of application **must** sell your qualifications.*

Imperative voice:
***Assure** the employer that you are the person for the job.*

Expression for giving advice:
***It's a good idea** to find out the name of a specific person to whom you can send your letter of application.*

Look back at the reading on pages 96–98. Find four additional examples in which the author gives advice. Try to write down one example for each of the following: **should**, **must**, the imperative voice, and an expression for giving advice.

1. _____

2. _____

3. _____

4. _____

Discussion & Writing

1. Imagine you are giving advice to a foreigner applying for a job in your country. Write a paragraph with four or five suggestions for things that he or she should do. Use as many different expressions for giving advice as you can.

2. In a letter of application, what would you list as your three best qualities? Think of at least one example to illustrate each quality. Share your ideas with a partner.

3. Find an advertisement for a job that looks interesting to you. Write a letter of application to this company. Follow the four principles outlined in the reading and use the letter on page 106 as a model.

2500 North Fruitridge Road
Springfield, IN 47811

March 1, 2001

Mr. John P. Storm, Vice President
Indiana Gas and Electric Company
1114 Broad Street
Terre Haute, IN 47815

Dear Mr. Storm:

Having served for the past several years as the administrative assistant of a private business, I would like to apply for the position of **executive assistant** which you advertised in the *Springfield Gazette* on Sunday, February 28, 2001.

As executive assistant to the Benlow Corporation in Terre Haute, I was directly responsible to Alba Jenkins, the company's owner. In addition to my administrative duties, I was responsible for scheduling all of Ms. Jenkins' appointments, screening her telephone calls and visitors, and organizing her paperwork and correspondence.

Essentially, I did everything I could to make Ms. Jenkins' heavy responsibilities easier. Thus, I am familiar with the duties of an executive assistant and believe I am prepared to anticipate and meet all your expectations. I am confident, too, that with enthusiasm and sincere effort, I can make the transition from a small business to a large corporation smoothly.

I would appreciate the opportunity to discuss my qualifications in person. I would be happy to come for an interview at your convenience, and I can be reached after 5 P.M. at 772-1248.

Sincerely yours,

Maria Smith

Maria Smith

Crossword Puzzle

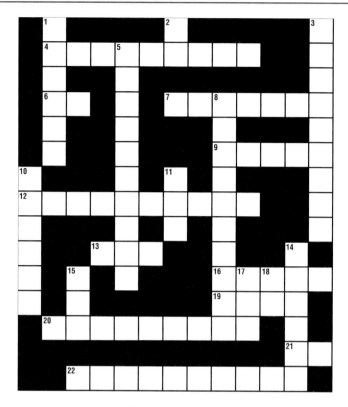

Use words from the reading to complete the crossword puzzle.

Across:

4 A résumé must be factual, ____, and brief. (line 26)

6 ____, your, his, her

7 The opening of a letter of application should be neither ____, nor unoriginal. (line 41)

9 You must persuade the employer to ____ you an interview. (line 3)

12 People who apply for a job are called job ____. (line 59)

13 ____ a question.

16 Another word for *short* is ____.

19 The opposite of *more* is ____.

20 A ____ letter is sent in response to a help-wanted ad. (line 11)

21 ____, you, him, her

22 A fact that can be checked is a ____ fact. (line 56)

Down:

1 A job you left is your ____ job. (line 35)

2 he, she, ____

3 A good letter of application will attract the reader's ____. (line 39)

5 The noun form of *enthusiastic* is ____.

8 The adjective form of *negotiate* is ____.

10 Employees are paid a ____.

11 ____, could; will, would

14 A letter of application should be sent with a ____. (line 6)

15 One plus one equals ____.

17 The Japanese flag is ____ and white.

18 ____, was; are, were

Mario Carreno, *La Siesta*

CONTENT:
The siesta tradition

READING SKILL:
Supporting details

BUILDING VOCABULARY:
Word forms

LANGUAGE FOCUS:
It's + adjective + infinitive

"*Oh Sleep!
It is a gentle thing.
Beloved from
pole to pole.[1]*"

*Samuel Coleridge
English poet
(1772 – 1834)*

---

[1] **from pole to pole**   from the North Pole to the South Pole

Chapter ▲ 10 Out To Lunch

Before You Read

1. The average workday in many countries is eight hours long. If you could work any hours of the day or night, which eight hours would you choose? Why?

2. Read the title of this article and then take one minute to skim it. What do you think the article will be about? Share your ideas with a partner.

3. Scan the article to find the information below.

   • What cities or countries are mentioned in this article?
   • How many people are mentioned in the article? What are their names?

4. In some countries it's a tradition to rest for an hour or two in the middle of the day. Why do you think this tradition exists? Share your ideas with a partner.

OUT TO LUNCH

*A big meal and a long nap is still a way
of life in Madrid.*

By Joe Robinson

from *Escape* magazine

1   Birds do it. Cats do it. And Spaniards most especially do it — every
day, in broad daylight. They nap. Grown adults — executives,
teachers, civil servants[2] — wink off[3] in the middle of the workday.
From 1 or 2 o'clock to 4:30 or so every afternoon, **Spain** stops the
5   world for a stroll[4] home, a leisurely meal, and a few z's.[5] **Common
Market** technocrats[6] have informed the Spanish that this is not the
way things will get done in a unified Europe.

At a time when productivity is the world's largest religion, the **siesta**
tradition lives on.[7] In Spain, work operates under the command of life,[8]
10   instead of the other way around. No task is so critical that it can't wait a
couple of hours while you attend to[9] more important matters like
eating, relaxing, or catching up on sleep. When the midday break hits,
offices empty[10] and streets clear. Befuddled foreigners quickly learn
that they have entered a new circadian order.[11]

15   "At first, I kept looking for things to do in the afternoon, and I just
couldn't believe that nothing was open," recalls Pier Roberts, an Oakland
writer who lived in Spain for several years. "I walked the streets of
Madrid looking for somewhere to go. It was a thousand degrees[12]
outside, you could see the heat waves, and it was like a ghost town.[13]"

---

[2] **civil servants**   government employees

[3] **wink off**   go to sleep

[4] **a stroll**   a leisurely walk

[5] **a few z's**   a nap; a short sleep

[6] **technocrats**   government experts in science and technology

[7] **lives on**   continues

[8] **work operates under the command of life**   working is less important
than living

[9] **attend to**   take care of; do

[10] **offices empty**   everyone leaves their office

[11] **a new circadian order**   a new way of organizing sleep and wake
patterns

[12] **a thousand degrees**   extremely hot

[13] **a ghost town**   an empty town; a town without people

20 Taking a long break in the middle of the day is not only healthier than the conventional lunch; it's apparently more natural. Sleep researchers have found that the Spanish biorhythm[14] may be tuned more closely to our biological clocks.[15] Studies suggest that humans are "biphasic" creatures, requiring days broken up by two periods of
25 sleep instead of one "monophasic" shift. The drowsiness you feel after lunch comes not from the food but from the time of day.

"All animals, including humans, have a biological rhythm," explains Claudio Stampi, director of the Chrono Biology Research Institute in Newton, Massachusetts. "One is a 24-hour rhythm — we
30 get tired by the end of the day and go to sleep — and there is a secondary peak of sleepiness and a decrease in alertness in the early afternoon. Some people have difficulty remaining awake, doing any sort of task between one and four in the afternoon. For others it's less difficult, but it's there. So there is a biological reason for siestas."

35 Unlike the average lunch break, the siesta is a true break in the action because there is no choice but to come to a full and complete stop. You can't do errands; the shops are closed. You can't make business calls; nobody's at the office. Most people go home for lunch, or get together with family or friends for a glass of wine and nod out[16]
40 afterwards.

The Spanish need their sleep. They've got a long night ahead of them, because another key component[17] of the siesta lifestyle is its nocturnal orbit.[18] After the afternoon work shift, from 4:30 to 8 p.m. or so, they may join friends for a drink. Dinner starts at 9 or 10 p.m.,
45 and from there it's out on the town[19] until one or two in the morning.

"It's a bad night in Madrid if you get home before six in the morning," laughs Roberts. The siesta's origins lie in climate and architecture. Like people in other places around the globe that are blast furnaces[20] much of the year, Spaniards turned to shade and stillness to avoid
50 incineration[21] in the middle of the day. At night, packed, simmering dwellings drove people into the streets to cool down.

---

[14] **biorhythm**   rhythm of life
[15] **biological clocks**   natural body rhythms
[16] **nod out**   go to sleep
[17] **key component**   important part
[18] **nocturnal orbit**   nighttime activity
[19] **out on the town**   having fun in town
[20] **blast furnaces**   very hot places
[21] **incineration**   burning up

While climate is still a factor, the siesta lifestyle today is driven primarily by the social imperative[22] of Spanish life, which places an equal if not greater emphasis on life outside the office. "We are not so obsessed only with work," says Florentino Sotomayor of the Spanish Tourist Board. "We take a break and have the opportunity of having coffee or beer with friends and thinking and talking about different issues, not only work."

55

About the Source

Escape magazine, published monthly in Santa Monica, California, features a wide range of advice and feature articles for the adventurous traveler. It focuses on unusual vacations to out-of-the-way places, eco-tourism, and outdoor adventure.

After You Read

Understanding the Text

A. **Multiple Choice.** For each item below, circle the answer that best completes each statement.

1. The main idea of this article is that _____.
   a. people everywhere should take naps
   b. napping is an important tradition in Spain
   c. it is important to have traditions
   d. the nightlife is exciting in Spain

2. During the midday break in Spain, people _____.
   a. go home for lunch
   b. do errands
   c. make business calls
   d. go shopping

---

[22] **social imperative** society's demands

3. The main idea of the fourth paragraph (lines 20–26) is that _____.

   a. the conventional lunch break is natural and healthy

   b. all animals have biological clocks

   c. food makes you feel drowsy

   d. it's natural for humans to nap

4. A biphasic creature needs _____.

   a. two sleep periods a day

   b. eight hours of sleep a day

   c. two days of sleep

   d. a long night of sleep

5. You can infer from the article that some businesspeople in other European countries _____.

   a. hope the siesta tradition will be introduced in their countries

   b. think the siesta tradition is impractical

   c. think that the siesta tradition will grow in popularity

   d. don't agree that napping is good for you

6. The overall tone of this article is _____.

   a. serious and academic

   b. light and silly

   c. light and informative

   d. scientific and technical

B. Consider the issues. *Work with a partner to answer the questions below.*

   1. In line 8, the writer claims that "productivity is the world's largest religion." What do you think he means by this? Do you agree? Why or why not?

   2. Each of the statements from the reading below is an exaggeration of the truth. Why do you think the author exaggerates the truth?

     • *It was a thousand degrees outside.*

     • *It's a bad night in Madrid if you get home before six in the morning.*

3. What do you think are the advantages and disadvantages of the siesta tradition? Add them to the chart below. Then decide if you think siestas are a good idea.

ADVANTAGES	DISADVANTAGES
You have more time to spend with your family.	

Reading Skill

Recognizing supporting details

Writers usually provide details and examples to support their ideas and opinions. Recognizing these supporting details will help you understand the writer's ideas.

Look back at the reading on pages 110–112 and find at least one detail that supports each of the ideas below.

IMPORTANT IDEAS	SUPPORTING DETAILS
1. For the Spanish, life is more important than work.	1. Going home for lunch is more important than staying at work.
2. The siesta is healthier and more natural than the average lunch break.	2.
3. Nightlife is an important part of Spanish social life.	3.

Building Vocabulary

Word forms

When you learn a new word, it's useful to learn other forms of the same word. You can find these forms in a dictionary.

A. Complete the chart below by adding the missing word forms. Then check your ideas by looking in a dictionary.

NOUN	ADJECTIVE
1. productivity	_____
2. drowsiness	_____
3. _____	leisurely
4. tradition	_____
5. _____	biological
6. difficulty	_____

B. Choose words from the chart in **A** to complete these sentences.

1. Some researchers think that people would be more _____ if they took a nap during the day.

2. Hot weather can make you _____.

3. Family life and _____ time are more important for many Spaniards than work.

4. A _____ lunch in Spain is long, relaxing, and delicious.

5. A reason for the siesta can be found in the science of _____.

6. It's _____ for many people to believe that in some countries, stores and businesses close for several hours during the middle of the day.

It's + adjective + infinitive
We often use *it's* + **adjective** + **infinitive** to give an opinion.

*Some people say **it's healthy to take** a nap in the afternoon.*
***It's fun to go out** on the town at night.*
***It's hard for me to get up** early in the morning.*

A. What's your opinion? Add an adjective to each sentence below to state your opinion.

1. It's _____ to go home for lunch.

2. I think it's _____ to take a nap in the afternoon.

3. In my opinion, it's _____ to stay out until six in the morning.

4. I would say that it's _____ to eat a big meal in the middle of the day.

5. In my country, it's _____ for people to leave work for the afternoon.

B. Complete these sentences with your own ideas. Then share your ideas with a partner.

1. Today it's common for young people to _____

   _____

2. I think it's easy to _____

   _____

3. If you want to learn a language, it's important to _____

   _____

4. In my opinion it's fun to _____

   _____

5. I believe that it is wrong to _____

   _____

A. Group work. Your traditions give information about your values, or what you believe is important. What do you think these traditions say about values?

- In Spain, it's a tradition to take a long lunch break so you can have a leisurely lunch with your family and take a nap.

- In Japan, it's a custom to take your shoes off before you enter a house.

- In the United States and other countries it is a tradition for men to give women flowers on birthdays, anniversaries, and other special occasions.

B. Work with several classmates to answer the questions below. Then share your group's answers with the class.

1. What is one of your culture's most important traditions? What does it say about your culture's values?

2. When you were a child, what was one of your favorite holiday traditions? Why did you like it?

3. What do these two quotations mean to you?

"A tradition without intelligence is not worth having."

—*T.S. Eliot (1888 –1965)*

"Tradition is a guide and not a jailer."

—*W. Somerset Maugham (1874 –1965)*

Crossword Puzzle

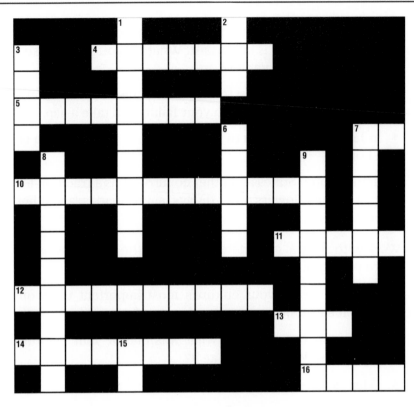

Use words from the reading to complete the crossword puzzle.

Across:

4 Water freezes at zero ___ centigrade. (line 18)

5 If you are ___ with something, you think about it all the time. (line 55)

7 ___, our; his, their

10 A ___ lunch break lasts about an hour. (line 21)

11 When you take a ___, you stop doing whatever you were doing.

12 Another word for *sleepiness* is ___. (line 25)

13 The opposite of *old* is ___.

14 In Spain, there are more hours of ___ in the summer than in the winter. (line 2)

16 The opposite of *go* is ___.

Down:

1 ___ means not rushed or hurried. (line 5)

2 The past tense of *feed* is ___.

3 hot, warm, ___, cold

6 A ___ town is completely empty. (line 19)

7 The ___ break in Spain is called the siesta. (line 12)

8 A ___ animal is active at night. (line 43)

9 For most people there is a decrease in ___ in the early afternoon. (line 31)

15 The opposite of *out* is ___.

Stephen Hawking—physicist, professor, and author

> "*The most beautiful thing we can experience is the mysterious. It is the source of all true art and science.*"

— *Albert Einstein*
German physicist
(1879 –1955)

Chapter Focus

CONTENT:
Talking about the importance of science

READING SKILL:
Finding main ideas

BUILDING VOCABULARY:
Keeping a vocabulary notebook

LANGUAGE FOCUS:
Using passive voice

Chapter ▲ 11 Public Attitudes Toward Science

Before You Read

1. In your opinion, what is the most important scientific discovery or invention?

2. Are you interested in science fiction movies or books? Are you interested in science itself? If so, which areas of science interest you the most?

3. Read the title of the essay on pages 122–124 and then take one minute to skim it. What do you think the essay is about? Share your ideas with a partner.

PUBLIC ATTITUDES TOWARD SCIENCE

by Stephen Hawking

from *Black Holes and Baby Universes*
and Other Essays

1   Whether we like it or not, the world we live in has changed a great
deal in the last hundred years, and it is likely to change even more in
the next hundred. Some people would like to stop these changes and
go back to what they see as a purer and simpler age. But as history
5   shows, the past was not that wonderful. It was not so bad for a
privileged minority,[1] though even they had to do without modern
medicine, and childbirth was highly risky for women. But for the vast
majority of the population, life was nasty and short.

Anyway, even if one wanted to, one couldn't put the clock back to
10   an earlier age. Knowledge and techniques can't just be forgotten. Nor
can one prevent further advances in the future. Even if all government
money for research were cut off, the force of competition would still
bring about advances in technology. Moreover, one cannot stop
inquiring minds[2] from thinking about basic science, whether or not
15   they were paid for it.

If we accept that we cannot prevent science and technology from
changing our world, we can at least try to ensure that the changes
they make are in the right directions. In a democratic society, this
means that the public needs to have a basic understanding of science,
20   so that it can make informed decisions and not leave them in the
hands of experts. At the moment, the public has a rather ambivalent
attitude toward science.[3] It has come to expect the steady increase in
the **standard of living** that new developments in science and
technology have brought to continue, but it also distrusts science
25   because it doesn't understand it. This distrust is evident in the
cartoon figure of the mad scientist working in his laboratory to
produce a **Frankenstein**. But the public also has a great interest in
science, as is shown by the large audiences for **science fiction**.

---

[1] **privileged minority**   small group of lucky people

[2] **inquiring minds**   people who are very interested in a topic

[3] **ambivalent attitude toward science**   liking certain aspects of
science and disliking others

What can be done to harness this interest[4] and give the public the scientific background it needs to make informed decisions on subjects like **acid rain**, the **greenhouse effect**, nuclear weapons, and **genetic engineering**? Clearly, the basis must lie in what is taught in schools. But in schools science is often presented in a dry and uninteresting manner. Children must learn it by rote[5] to pass examinations, and they don't see its relevance to the world around them. Moreover, science is often taught in terms of equations. Although equations are a concise and accurate way of describing mathematical ideas, they frighten most people.

Scientists and engineers tend to express their ideas in the form of equations because they need to know the precise value of quantities. But for the rest of us, a qualitative grasp of[6] scientific concepts is sufficient, and this can be conveyed by words and diagrams, without the use of equations.

The science people learn in school can provide the basic framework.[7] But the rate of scientific progress is now so rapid that there are always new developments that have occurred since one was at school or university. I never learned about molecular biology or transistors[8] at school, but genetic engineering and computers are two of the developments most likely to change the way we live in the future. Popular books and magazine articles about science can help to put across new developments, but even the most successful popular book is read by only a small proportion of the population. There are some very good science programs on TV, but others present scientific wonders simply as magic, without explaining them or showing how they fit into the framework of scientific ideas. Producers of television science programs should realize that they have a responsibility to educate the public, not just entertain it.

What are the science-related issues that the public will have to make decisions on in the near future? By far the most urgent is that of nuclear weapons. Other global problems, such as food supply or the greenhouse effect, are relatively slow-acting, but a nuclear war could mean the end of all human life on earth within days. The relaxation of **East-West tensions** has meant that the fear of nuclear war has

---

[4] **harness this interest**   use this interest
[5] **learn by rote**   learn by repeating the same thing many times
[6] **qualitative grasp of**   general understanding of
[7] **basic framework**   general facts and ideas on a topic
[8] **transistors**   small electronic parts in radios and TVs

receded from public consciousness.[9] But the danger is still there as
65　long as there are enough weapons to kill the entire population of the
world many times over. Nuclear weapons are still poised to strike[10]
all the major cities in the Northern Hemisphere.[11] It would only take a
computer error to trigger[12] a global war.

　　If we manage to avoid a nuclear war, there are still other dangers
70　that could destroy us all. There's a sick joke[13] that the reason we have
not been contacted by an alien civilization[14] is that civilizations tend
to destroy themselves when they reach our stage.[15] But I have
sufficient faith in the good sense of the public to believe that we
might prove this wrong.

About the **Author**

Stephen Hawking (1942–　　) is a physicist, professor at Cambridge
University in England, and author of the award-winning book, ***A Brief
History of Time***. Hawking studies black holes, the big bang theory,
and other scientific mysteries of the universe.

---

[9] **receded from public consciousness**　left people's everyday thoughts
[10] **poised to strike**　ready to attack
[11] **Northern Hemisphere**　the portion of the Earth north of the Equator
[12] **trigger**　start
[13] **sick joke**　story that makes fun of serious topics like death
[14] **alien civilization**　people from another planet
[15] **our stage**　our level of scientific development

After You Read

A. **Multiple choice.** For each item below, circle the best answer.

1. History shows that, in the past, life was _____.
   a. not so bad
   b. comfortable for most people
   c. hard for most people
   d. easier for women

2. Advances in science and technology _____.
   a. can be forgotten very quickly
   b. can't be stopped by cutting government support
   c. can be stopped by cutting government support
   d. should be controlled by scientists and engineers

3. The public feels _____.
   a. ambivalent toward science
   b. completely positive about science
   c. completely negative about science
   d. negative about science fiction

4. If you understand the general principles of science, even though you are not good at mathematics, you have a _____ grasp of scientific concepts.
   a. quantitative
   b. qualitative
   c. precise
   d. rote

5. Science programs on TV should _____.
   a. present a lot of equations
   b. focus on science fiction
   c. show science as a kind of magic
   d. educate the public, as well as entertain

6. The most urgent science-related issue today is _____.

    a. the greenhouse effect

    b. acid rain

    c. genetic engineering

    d. nuclear weapons

B. Consider the issues. Work with a partner to answer the questions below.

  1. According to the author, what are the basic reasons people don't like science? Do you agree with the reasons he gives? Why or why not?

  2. What are some of the ways the author feels people can educate themselves on scientific issues?

  3. The author writes, "The world has changed a great deal in the last hundred years, and it is likely to change even more in the next hundred." What are one or two scientific discoveries that you think will be made during your lifetime?

Reading Skill

Understanding main ideas
A **main idea** is a message the writer wants to communicate about the topic. Writers don't always state their main ideas directly. Sometimes, writers imply or suggest their main ideas.

A. What does the author think? Put a check (√) next to the sentences that Stephen Hawking would agree with.

  1. _____ Life was better in the old days.

  2. _____ There are various ways the public can be educated about science so they can make informed decisions about important issues.

3. _____ The media can educate people about the most recent developments in technology.

4. _____ The only way to understand scientific concepts is by mastering mathematical equations.

5. _____ Only scientists and engineers can protect the world from environmental disasters.

6. _____ The science people learn in school can provide a basic framework for scientific understanding.

B. **Find the main idea.** Now look at the ideas you checked above. Which is the **most** important idea in the reading? In other words, which idea expresses the author's main idea? Write an **M** next to that idea to show it's the **main idea**.

C. **Find supporting details.** Now look at the other sentences you checked in **A**. Which of the ideas support the main idea? Write an **S** next to those ideas to show they are **supporting details**.

D. Can you find any other ideas in the reading that support the main idea? Write them below.

_____

_____

_____

_____

_____

Building Vocabulary

Keeping a vocabulary notebook
When you hear or read a new word or phrase that's important to you, add it to your **vocabulary notebook.** Try grouping the words and phrases in your notebook by topic. Next to each item, write down a sentence containing the word that will help you remember the word's meaning.

A. Look back at the reading and find three words or expressions that are related to science. Add these to the chart below.

B. If you are not sure of the meaning, look up the word in your dictionary. Then write a sentence of your own beside each word to help you remember its meaning.

WORDS OR EXPRESSIONS	SENTENCES
greenhouse effect	The greenhouse effect refers to the way that the atmosphere around the Earth acts like the glass ceiling in a greenhouse.
1.	
2.	
3.	

Using passive voice

The passive voice is formed with the verb *be* + a past participle.

is/are done   was/were done
is/are being done   has/have been done
will
can/could
should   be done
might/may
must

The passive voice is used when:

(1) The doer of the action is unknown or unknowable:

> The Earth **could be destroyed** *in an instant.*
> *My car* **was stolen** *during the night.*

(2) The doer of the action is less important than the action itself:

> Gone with the Wind **was written** *by Margaret Mitchell.*

A. The sentences below are from the article. Read the sentences and underline any verbs or verb phrases in the passive voice you find.

Example: Knowledge and techniques <u>can't just be forgotten</u>.

1. In schools science is often presented in a dry and uninteresting manner.

2. Moreover, science is often taught in terms of equations.

3. One cannot stop inquiring minds from thinking about basic science, whether or not they were paid for it.

4. Popular books and magazine articles about science can help to put across new developments, but even the most successful popular book is read by only a small proportion of the population.

5. Even if all the government money for research were cut off, the force of competition would still bring about advances in technology.

6. There's a sick joke that the reason we have not been contacted by an alien civilization is that civilizations tend to destroy themselves when they reach our stage.

B. Look again at the passive voice verbs you underlined in **A**. Why do you think the writer used the passive in each of these cases? For each verb, choose one of the explanations from the *using passive voice* box above to explain the reason.

1. What are two or three important science-related problems or questions facing your country or region of the world? Which of these problems or questions is the most serious? How should this issue be addressed?

2. Why are people interested in science fiction? Why do you think some people might dislike science but really enjoy science fiction books and movies? Share your ideas with a partner.

3. **A.** Choose the science-related question below that interests you the most:

   • How is the Internet changing our lives?

   • What is the most important invention of the past 50 years?

   • Who is the greatest person in the history of science?

   • When will scientists find a cure for _____?
     (Choose a disease like cancer or AIDS.)

   B. Prepare a five-minute presentation that addresses your question. Use this outline to help you:

INTRODUCTION

"My name is _____ and I am delighted to be here today. I'd like to speak to you about . . ."

ORGANIZATION

"I have divided my talk into three parts . . ."

MAIN PARTS

1. *"First . . ."*

2. *"That brings me to . . ."*

3. *"Finally . . ."*

CONCLUSION

"In closing . . ."

Crossword Puzzle

Use words from the reading to complete the crossword puzzle.

Across:

4 Another way to say *correct* is ___.

6 A synonym for *very fast* is ___. (line 45)

9 Television programs can entertain and ___. (line 57)

11 The noun form of *compete* is ___.

14 is, ___; was, were

15 I, me; we, ___

16 Another way to say *a lot* is a great ___. (line 2)

17 ___, lay, lain

18 Another word for *hit* is ___. (line 66)

19 An ___ decision is based on good information. (line 20)

Down:

1 *Star Wars* and *Star Trek* are of science ___ films. (line 28)

2 The past form of *pay* is ___.

3 Another word for a *thought* is an ___.

5 me, you, him, her, us, ___

7 Another word for *exact* is ___. (line 40)

8 If you have enough of something, you have a ___ amount. (line 42)

10 Another word for *in addition* is ___. (line 13)

12 The simple past of the verb *occur* is ___.

13 E = mc² is an example of an ___. (line 36)

CONTENT:
Marriage customs

*BUILDING
VOCABULARY:*
Synonyms/adjectives
and adverbs

READING SKILL:
Inferencing

LANGUAGE FOCUS:
Subjunctive verbs

*"To the man who has
conquered the bride's
heart and her
mother's."*

— *Traditional wedding toast*

Chapter 12 ▲ John's Taiwanese Wedding

Before You Read

1. The photographs on page 132 illustrate scenes from the story you are going to read. What is happening in the photographs?

2. In the story, a Taiwanese woman and an American man are going to get married. What problems might they have planning their wedding ceremony?

3. Can you guess from the title what kind of story it is? Biographical? Autobiographical? Humorous? How do you know?

JOHN'S TAIWANESE WEDDING

by John Felty and Bill McDowell

from *Hemispheres Magazine*

1   In the spring, Huiling's mother pulled me aside and asked, "What exactly are your plans with my daughter?" As I had already discussed marriage with Huiling, my 24-year-old Taiwanese fiancée, Mrs. Chen's tone didn't fluster[1] me. She was just worried that if I, a 29-year-old
5   American **graduate student**, didn't have serious marital intentions,[2] her family would suffer a great loss of face.[3] One point that infuriated[4] her was my inability to find a *meiren*.

I asked some friends about a *meiren* and learned that it's a title given to the groom's relative who goes to the prospective[5] bride's
10   house to carry out all the touchy[6] negotiations that go into planning a traditional Chinese wedding. Having a *meiren* is a little old-fashioned, but it can be useful. As a third party,[7] they help save face during the arguments that inevitably arise over issues like the **dowry** amount and how many "marriage cakes" to buy, which are sent to
15   relatives and friends to announce the engagement. One could easily spend $6,000 on these cakes alone. Determined to make the Chens proud to have a foreign son-in-law, I searched for a *meiren*.

I work as an Asian representative of a British company, so I asked my boss, Mr. Lin to suggest a *meiren*. He recommended that I ask Mr.
20   Wu, who works at my company. He was delighted to assist, assuring me he would need only a small "red envelope." Huiling later explained that red envelopes are used for **cash gifts** at ceremonies and on holidays, and a *meiren* generally gets $500–$1000.

The next day, Mr. Lin burst out of a meeting grinning broadly,
25   patting one of our customers on the back. "Mr. Ou has agreed to be

---

[1] **fluster**   bother; upset

[2] **marital intentions**   plans to get married

[3] **suffer a loss of face**   lose the respect of other people

[4] **infuriated**   angered

[5] **prospective**   likely to be

[6] **touchy**   sensitive

[7] **a third party**   someone who is not personally involved in the negotiations

your *meiren*. He will do much better than Mr. Wu, who is too soft and easygoing.[8] Mr. Ou will give you big face[9] and ensure your girlfriend's parents give you lots of things." With growing interest, I asked, "What kinds of things?" "Their house, car, their money, that kind of stuff," Mr. Ou explained confidently. "Don't I need to give them money?" I asked. "You only give them money if you don't know what you're doing," confided Mr. Ou.

Later I asked my boss about using Mr. Wu as a *meiren* after all, as he seemed a little more conventional[10]... "Oh, Mr. Wu will be there, too," he said offhandedly. I was confused. Why both? "You can't just come with one person," he explained. When asked how many people I needed, Mr. Lin replied casually, "Six, but 12 is better."

Huiling assured me that 6 and 12 are lucky numbers, and in a traditional and formal engagement I would need either number of people. This sure seemed extravagant,[11] but I was determined to do things the Taiwanese way.

It took a week to build my team of *meiren*. My boss, Mr. Lin, reluctantly agreed. Mr. Ou recruited his business partner. And there was Mr. Chen, from our sales department. With Messrs.[12] Ou and Wu, I had five *meiren*, so I cajoled Mr. Ou to[13] sign on one of his old customers. I barely knew him, but he looked distinguished.[14] I had my *meiren* team at last!

I proudly stopped by Huiling's parents' house to make the date. "Six people will be coming by with me next Monday to visit with you, can you be here?" They seemed pleased with the news and told me they'd be ready. The next day I called Huiling to make sure she'd have the best tea and fruit for the guests. I heard her mother ask in the background, "Why does he want to bring all those friends, anyway?"

"They're not friends, they're *meiren*," I told Huiling. "Why in the world are you bringing six *meiren*?" she exclaimed. I swallowed hard.[15] "To negotiate. To talk to your folks. I don't know, it's your custom!" I heard Mrs. Chen again shouting in the background, "What

---

[8] **easygoing**   not easily disturbed or irritated; easy to please

[9] **give you big face**   a direct translation from the Chinese meaning 'will make you look important'

[10] **conventional**   traditional; like other people

[11] **extravagant**   excessive; too generous

[12] **Messrs.**   plural of *Mr.*

[13] **cajoled Mr. Ou to**   used humor to persuade Mr. Ou to

[14] **distinguished**   important and respected

[15] **I swallowed hard.**   I waited before I said anything.

meiren? Six *meiren*? Who ever heard of that? What am I supposed to say to all of them? Six! That's crazy!" I was losing my cool.[16] "You said 60 six. Everybody said six! I booked six!"

Huiling replied evenly,[17] "Listen, you need six people, but only one *meiren*. Now count. I'm one person, Mom and Dad make three, one *meiren*, and a friend and you make six. But don't worry. My parents decided not to bother about a *meiren*."

65 Our *meiren* scenario illustrates how easily communication in a cross-cultural relationship can become muddled.[18] Due to my imperfect Mandarin and my inexperience with Taiwanese customs, I confused the need for six people with the need for six *meiren*.

The highlight of the wedding was the 12-course Chinese feast at a 70 local restaurant. As is the custom, Huiling and I, with parents in tow,[19] stopped at each of the 23 tables and **toasted** my new relatives. My parents couldn't understand the words, but shared in the outpouring of good wishes for a bright future.

About the **Authors**

John Felty came to Taiwan as a graduate student in Asian Political Systems. He and his wife Huiling now live in Colorado.
Bill McDowell is a photographer and professor in Texas.

---

[16] **I was losing my cool.** I was becoming upset.

[17] **evenly** calmly

[18] **muddled** confused

[19] **in tow** following behind

After You Read

Understanding the Text

A. **True, False, or Impossible to Know?** Read the sentences below and write T (True), F (False), or I (Impossible to Know).

_____ 1. At the beginning of the story, John doesn't want to marry Mrs. Chen's daughter.

_____ 2. At first, John doesn't know what a *meiren* is or how to find one.

_____ 3. John asks Huiling to help him find a *meiren*.

_____ 4. Mr. Lin recommends more than one person to be John's *meiren*.

_____ 5. John needs six *meiren* for the wedding negotiations.

_____ 6. John and Huiling's wedding ceremony included both Taiwanese and American customs.

B. **Consider the issues.** Work with a partner to answer the questions below.

1. At the beginning of the story, what is John's problem? What does he do to solve his problem?

2. What mistake does John make? What are the consequences of his mistake?

3. What is the reason for the misunderstanding in this story?

4. The words *marriage cakes* (line 14) and *red envelope* (line 21) appear in quotation marks (" ") in the story. Why do you think that is?

Inferencing

When you make an **inference,** you make a judgment based on the evidence. Readers often make inferences about the characters in a story based on their words and actions (the evidence). For example, in the story on pages 134–136, you can infer that John wants to please Mrs. Chen. You can make this inference based on the fact that John tries very hard to do what Mrs. Chen wants.

What can you infer about the characters in the story? Read the evidence below and write an inference.

1. In the story, John asks his friends for information about Taiwanese customs. What can you infer about his friends?

_____

2. John goes to his boss for help in finding a *meiren.* What can you infer about his boss from this?

_____

3. Mr. Lin says that Mr. Wu is too soft and easygoing and that Mr. Ou would be a better *meiren.* What can you infer about Mr. Ou?

_____

4. John wants the Chens to be proud to have a foreign son-in-law. What does this tell you about John?

_____

5. John's parents can't understand what Huiling's parents are saying at the wedding. What can you infer about John's parents?

_____

Synonyms
Synonyms are words that are similar in meaning. For example, *glad* and *happy* are synonyms.

A. Synonyms. Number the paragraphs in the reading on pages 134–136 from 1 to 12. Then find the words below.

1. In paragraph 1, find a synonym for the word *since*.

_____

2. In paragraph 1, find a word that means *angered*.

_____

3. In paragraph 2, which word means *out of date?*

_____

4. In paragraph 3, find a synonym for *supervisor*.

_____

5. In paragraph 4, find a word that means *smiling*.

_____

6. In paragraph 7, which word is a synonym for *group?*

_____

7. In paragraph 8, find a word that means *happy*.

_____

Adjectives and adverbs

Many words have both an adjective and an adverb form. Learning them together will help build your vocabulary.

B. Adjectives and Adverbs. What are the missing adjectives and adverbs in the box below? Write your ideas. Then look for the words in the story on pages 134–136 and check your spelling.

ADJECTIVES	ADVERBS
1. confident	confidently
2. casual	
3.	easily
4. inevitable	
5. offhanded	
6.	proudly
7. reluctant	
8.	softly

C. Complete each sentence with a word from the box above. More than one answer may be possible.

1. It is probably _____ that you will have communication problems when you are speaking with a foreigner.

2. It's not appropriate to dress _____ for a wedding.

3. It's not always _____ to do the right thing.

4. If someone is _____ to answer a personal question, you probably shouldn't insist.

5. If this course is too _____, you should find a harder one.

6. I'd be _____ to represent my country in the Olympics.

7. It's important to speak _____ when you give a speech.

Subjunctive Verbs

The verbs below are often followed by a noun clause. Note that the verb in each noun clause is in the simple form.

advise	*insist*	*propose*	*request*
demand	*suggest*	*recommend*	*require*

Mr. Lin *suggested* that John **use** Mr. Wu as his *meiren.*
John *requested* that Mr. Lin **be** one of his *meiren*.

A. Complete the sentences below with information from the story. More than one answer may be possible.

1. Taiwanese wedding customs *require* that a couple
   _____ "marriage cakes" to relatives and friends to announce the engagement.

2. At first, Mr. Lin *recommended* that John _____ Mr. Wu to be his *meiren*.

3. Later, Mr. Lin *suggested* that Mr. Ou _____ John's *meiren*.

4. Mr. Lin *requested* that John _____ him a small "red envelope".

5. John *suggested* that Huiling _____ the best tea for their six guests.

6. Mrs. Chen *demanded* that John not _____ six *meiren*.

B. Complete these sentences with your own ideas. Then share your ideas with a partner.

1. Doctors usually *recommend* that someone with a very high fever

   _____

2. Our teacher *insists* that each student _____

   _____

3. When I was a child, my parents *insisted* that I _____

_____

4. My country *requires* that a citizen _____

_____

5. The post office *requires* that a letter _____

_____

6. I would refuse if someone *demanded* that I _____

_____

Discussion & Writing

1. Imagine that a foreigner asked you the questions below about wedding traditions in your country. How would you answer?

   a. Is it important to give a gift when someone gets married? If so, what's a good gift and when should you give it?

   b. What should guests wear to a wedding?

   c. What things would be rude to do at a wedding?

   d. How long does a wedding celebration last?

2. Write a list of wedding dos and don'ts for a foreigner who is planning to marry a friend of yours.

Crossword Puzzle

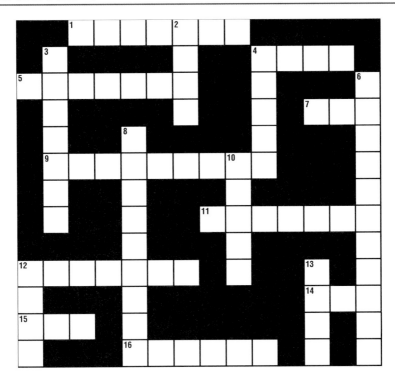

Use words from the reading to complete the crossword puzzle.

Across:

1 At the beginning of the story, Huiling is John's ___. (line 3)
4 tell, told; ___, found
5 John and Huiling had a wedding feast with 12 ___. (line 69)
7 The word ___ means *also*.
9 John's Mandarin is ___. (line 67)
11 Two people get engaged when they are planning to get ___.
12 The writer works for a ___ company in Taiwan. (line 18)
14 The opposite of *in* is ___.
15 Three plus three equals ___.
16 Summer, fall, winter, ___.

Down:

2 In Taiwan, red envelopes are used for ___ gifts. (line 22)
3 Another word for *concerned* is ___. (line 4)
4 John wants Huiling to serve tea and ___ to his guests. (line 52)
6 A person who feels sure he or she is right speaks ___. (line 30)
8 Usually a *meiren* is one of the groom's ___. (line 71)
10 Mrs. Chen thought it was ___ to bring six meiren to her house. (line 59)
12 Mr. Lin is the writer's ___.
13 The opposite of *bad* is ___.

Leonardo da Vinci (1452–1519)

> **"Genius is the capacity to see ten things where the ordinary man sees one."**

— *Ezra Pound*
American poet and writer
(1885 –1972)

Chapter Focus

CONTENT:
Understanding how geniuses think

READING SKILL:
Finding examples that help explain new ideas

BUILDING VOCABULARY:
Grouping words

LANGUAGE FOCUS:
Understanding the use of colons

13 The Art of Genius

Before You Read

1. Read the definition of the word *genius* below. Identify someone whom you consider a genius. Why is he or she a genius? Share your reasons with a partner.

> **genius**/ˈdʒiːniəs/ *n* (*pl.* **geniuses**) **1** an exceptionally great mental or creative ability: *a writer of genius.* **2** a person who has such ability: *Einstein was a mathematical genius.*

2. Read the title of the article on page 146 and then take one minute to skim it. What do you think the article is about? Share your ideas with a partner.

3. Scan the article and circle the names of people mentioned. Who are they? What do they have in common?

4. What do you know about the people mentioned below? With a partner, add any information you can to the chart. Then, read the article to fill in more information.[1]

NAME	LIVED WHEN?	FAMOUS FOR WHAT?
Galileo Galilei	1564–1642	scientist; invented the telescope
Wolfgang Amadeus Mozart		
Sigmund Freud		
Leonardo da Vinci		
Albert Einstein		

---

[1] If you need some help completing the chart, review the Culture Notes for this chapter.

THE ART OF GENIUS: SIX WAYS
TO THINK LIKE EINSTEIN

by Michael Michalko

from *The Futurist/Utne Reader*

1   How do geniuses come up with ideas? What links the thinking style that produced ***Mona Lisa*** with the one that spawned[2] the **theory of relativity**? What can we learn from the thinking strategies of the **Galileos**, **Edisons**, and **Mozarts** of history?

5   For years, scholars tried to study genius by analyzing statistics. In 1904, Havelock Ellis noted that most geniuses were fathered by men older than 30, had mothers younger than 25, and usually were sickly children. Other researchers reported that many were celibate[3] (**Descartes**), fatherless (**Dickens**), or motherless (**Darwin**). In the
10   end, the data illuminated[4] nothing.

     Academics also tried to measure the links between intelligence and genius. But they found that run-of-the-mill[5] physicists had **IQs** much higher than **Nobel Prize** winner and extraordinary genius **Richard Feynman**, whose IQ was a merely respectable 122. Genius
15   is not about mastering 14 languages at the age of seven or even being especially smart. Creativity is not the same as intelligence.

     Most people of average intelligence can figure out the expected conventional response[6] to a given problem. For example, when asked "What is one-half of 13?" most of us immediately answer six and one-
20   half. That's because we tend to think *reproductively*. When confronted with a problem, we sift through what we've been taught and what has worked for us in the past, select the most promising approach, and work toward the solution.

     Geniuses, on the other hand, think *productively*. They ask: "How
25   many different ways can I look at this problem?" and "How many

----

[2] **spawned**   gave birth to; was responsible for

[3] **celibate**   not active sexually

[4] **illuminated**   showed; proved

[5] **run-of-the-mill**   ordinary

[6] **conventional response**   typical answer

ways can I solve it?" A productive thinker, for example, would find a number of ways to "halve 13"[7]:

6.5
1/3 = 1 and 3
THIR TEEN = 4
XI/II[8] = 11 and 2

The mark of genius[9] is the willingness to explore *all* the alternatives, not just the most likely solution. Reproductive thinking fosters rigidity.[10] This is why we often fail when we're confronted with a new problem that appears on the surface to be similar to others we've solved, but is, in fact, significantly different. Interpreting a problem through your past experience will inevitably lead you astray.[11] If you think the way you've always thought, you'll get what you've always gotten.

For centuries, the Swiss dominated the watch industry. But in 1968, when a U.S. inventor unveiled[12] a battery-powered watch at the World Watch Congress, every Swiss watch manufacturer rejected it because it didn't fit their limited paradigm.[13] Meanwhile, Seiko, a Japanese electronics company, took one look at the invention and proceeded to change the future of the world watch market.

By studying the notebooks, correspondence, and conversations of some of the world's great thinkers in science, art, and industry, scholars have identified the following thinking strategies that enable geniuses to generate original ideas:

1. Geniuses look at problems from all angles.[14] **Sigmund Freud's** analytical methods were designed to find details that didn't fit traditional paradigms in order to come up with a completely new point of view. To solve a problem creatively, you must abandon the first approach that comes to mind,

---

[7] **halve 13**   divide 13 into two equal parts

[8] **XI/II**   See *Culture Note* for **Roman numerals**

[9] **mark of genius**   true sign that someone is a genius

[10] **fosters rigidity**   leads to uncreative thinking

[11] **lead you astray**   take you in the wrong direction

[12] **unveiled**   showed for the first time

[13] **paradigm**   model that shows how something works

[14] **look at something from all angles**   think about something from many different perspectives

55 which usually stems from past experience, and reconceptualize the problem.[15] Geniuses do not merely solve existing problems; they identify new ones.

2. Geniuses make their thought visible. Geniuses develop visual and spatial abilities that allow them to display information
60 in new ways. The explosion of creativity in the **Renaissance** was tied to the development of graphic illustration during that period, notably the scientific diagrams of **Leonardo da Vinci** and Galileo Galilei. Galileo revolutionized science by making his thought graphically visible while his contemporaries[16] used
65 more conventional means.

3. Geniuses produce. Thomas Edison held 1,093 patents,[17] still a record. He guaranteed a high level of productivity by giving himself idea quotas:[18] one minor invention every 10 days and a major invention every six months. **Johann Sebastian Bach**
70 wrote a cantata[19] every week, even when he was sick or exhausted. Wolfgang Mozart produced more than 600 pieces of music.

4. Geniuses make novel combinations. Like playful children with buckets of building blocks,[20] geniuses constantly
75 combine and recombine ideas, images, and thoughts. The laws of heredity[21] were developed by **Gregor Mendel**, who combined mathematics and biology to create a new science of genetics.

5. Geniuses force relationships. Their facility[22] to connect
80 the unconnected enables geniuses to see things others miss. Da Vinci noticed the similarity between the sound of a bell and a stone hitting water - and concluded that sound travels in waves.

---

[15] **reconceptualize the problem** find creative new ways to think about and solve the problem

[16] **contemporaries** people who lived at the same time as Galileo

[17] **held patents** owned the rights to new inventions

[18] **idea quota** minimum number of new ideas within a certain time period

[19] **cantata** piece of religious music with singing

[20] **building blocks** small pieces of wood that children play with

[21] **heredity** scientific process of passing qualities from parents to children

[22] **facility** ability to do something well

6. Geniuses prepare themselves for chance. Whenever we attempt to do something and fail, we end up doing something else. That's the first principle of creative accident. We may ask ourselves why we have failed to do what we intended, which is a reasonable question. But the creative accident leads to the question: What have we done? Answering that one in a novel, unexpected way is the essential creative act. It is not luck, but creative insight of the highest order.[23]

This may be the most important lesson of all: When you find something interesting, drop everything and go with it. Too many talented people fail to make significant leaps of imagination because they've become fixated on their pre-conceived plan.[24] But not the truly great minds. They don't wait for gifts of chance; they make them happen.

About the Source

Utne Reader is a bi-monthly magazine that publishes articles from over 2,000 sources. Subtitled "The Best of the Alternative Media," Utne Reader covers topics including race, feminism, environment, global politics, art, media, humor, relationships and in-depth news.

---

[23] **highest order**   highest level or quality

[24] **become fixated on their pre-conceived plan**   are only able to think about their original plan

After You Read

Understanding the Text

A. **True or False.** Read the sentences below and write T (True) or F (False).

_____ 1. The author's main purpose is to discuss the importance of 12 famous geniuses.

_____ 2. The author would agree that all geniuses are creative.

_____ 3. Geniuses always have an exceptionally high IQ.

_____ 4. Most people are reproductive thinkers.

_____ 5. According to the article, geniuses are identified by their ability to solve problems much faster than average people.

_____ 6. Geniuses have little patience for accidents.

B. **Consider the issues.** Work with a partner to answer the questions below.

1. How are geniuses different from the rest of the population? What special abilities or skills do geniuses have that other people don't?

2. The author outlines six "thinking strategies" that help geniuses develop original ideas. In your opinion, which of these strategies is most important to the success of a scientist? An artist? A businessperson? Why?

3. The reading refers to 12 famous geniuses, all of whom are European or North American men. Make a list of three men or women whom you consider to be geniuses from your culture. Explain why each person is a genius.

Finding examples that help explain new ideas
Writers use examples to help readers remember new ideas.
Finding and thinking about specific examples can help you
understand and remember important ideas in a reading.

Complete the chart below with examples that support each idea from
the reading. Then share your ideas with a partner.

IDEAS ABOUT GENIUSES
• They try to solve problems in as many different ways as possible.
Example: Finding five or more ways to divide 13 in half.
• They open their minds to new ways of thinking about things.
Example:
• They creatively combine two or more things or ideas to make something new.
Example:
• They create a large quantity of things or ideas.
Example:

Grouping words
Putting words in groups helps you learn and remember them.

1. Review the following adjectives used to describe people in the reading on pages 146–148. Put each word in the correct column in the chart below:

average	talented	original	conventional
playful	creative	run-of-the-mill	extraordinary

GENIUSES	ORDINARY PEOPLE

2. Now add three of your own adjectives to each column in the chart above. Share your ideas with a partner.

3. The adjectives in the chart are used to describe people. Can any of these adjectives also be used to describe things? Places?

Understanding the use of colons
A **colon** (:) can be used to introduce (1) a quotation, (2) a list of information, or (3) an important statement or question.

To introduce a quotation
Geniuses think *productively*. They ask: "How many different ways can I look at this problem?"

To introduce a list of information
A productive thinker, for example, would find a number of ways to "halve 13:"

> 6.5
> 1/3 = 1 and 3
> THIR TEEN = 4
> XI/II = 11 and 2

To introduce an important statement or question
But the creative accident leads to the question: What have we done?

1. Look back at the reading and underline two additional examples of the use of a colon. Why did the author use a colon in each of these cases?

2. Complete the following sentences with your own ideas.

   a. When swimming in the ocean, you need to remember this:

   _____

   _____.

   b. It's a good idea to pack the following five things for a vacation in Hawaii: _____

   _____.

   c. After a terrible argument with his mother, John turned to her and said: _____

   _____.

A. Form a group of three or four and place six pens of the same size on a table in front of you. Try the following:

1. Arrange the pens so that they form two equal triangles.

2. Now, arrange the pens so that they form four triangles of any size.

3. Next, make four triangles of equal size.

4. Finally, use these six pens to make eight triangles of any size.

Was this activity difficult for you? Why or why not?

B. 1. How does each of the quotations below relate to ideas in this chapter?

> *"Genius is one percent inspiration and ninety–nine percent perspiration."*
>
> — *Thomas Edison, American inventor (1847–1931)*
>
> *"Imagination is more important than knowledge."*
> — *Albert Einstein, German-American physicist (1879 –1955)*
>
> *"Never be afraid to sit awhile and think."*
> — *Lorraine Hansberry, American playwright (1930 –1965)*

2. Select a famous genius and research information on his or her life. Why is this person considered a genius? What is his or her greatest contribution to the world? Share your findings with your classmates.

Crossword Puzzle

Use words from the reading to complete the crossword puzzle.

Across:

3 A very knowledgeable person who has done advanced study in a subject can be called a ___. (line 5)

4 make, made; have, ___

10 Most people tend to think ___. (line 20)

12 ___, or, but

15 A person from Switzerland is ___.

17 *Standard* and *typical* are synonyms for ___. (line 65)

18 me, my; ___, your

Down:

1 ___, what, where, when, why

2 The noun form of *productive* is ___. (line 67)

5 Geniuses look at problems from all ___. (line 50)

6 Someone who doesn't have a father is ___. (line 9)

7 A new or unusual idea is a ___ idea. (line 73)

8 Gregor Mendel developed the laws of ___. (line 76)

9 When you solve a problem, you come up with a ___. (line 33)

11 Numerical facts are called ___. (line 5)

13 live, lived; is, ___

14 A ___ person is someone who is often unwell. (line 7)

16 The past form of *tie* is ___.

Chapter Focus

CONTENT:
Conversational styles

READING SKILL:
Identifying organizational patterns

BUILDING VOCABULARY:
Prefixes

LANGUAGE FOCUS:
Conditionals

"If you're going to play the game properly, you'd better know every rule."

— Barbara Jordan
American politician
(1936 –1996)

Chapter ▲ 14 Conversational Ball Games

Before You Read

1. Which statements describe the game of tennis? Which describe bowling? Write T (tennis) or B (bowling).

   _____ a. To play, you need a ball and ten pins.

   _____ b. For this game, you need a ball, a racquet, and a net.

   _____ c. Players hit the ball back and forth to each other.

   _____ d. If you miss the ball, your opponent gets a point.

2. What else do you know about tennis and bowling? Share information with a partner.

3. Read the questions below. Then look over pages 158–160 to find answers to the questions.

   a. What is the title of the article? Based on the title, what do you think the article is about?

   b. Who is the author of the article? What do you think the author's nationality is? Why?

   c. What is the topic of the article?

4. The author of the article makes the two statements below. As you read the article, underline any examples she gives to support these statements.

   > "A Western-style conversation between two people is like a game of tennis."

   > "A Japanese-style conversation... is like bowling."

CONVERSATIONAL BALL GAMES

by Nancy Masterson Sakamoto

from *Polite Fictions — Why Japanese and
Americans Seem Rude to Each Other*

1   After I was married and had lived in **Japan** for a while, my Japanese
gradually improved to the point where I could take part in simple
conversations with my husband and his friends and family. And I
began to notice that often, when I joined in, the others would look
5   startled, and the conversational topic would come to a halt.[1] After
this happened several times, it became clear to me that I was doing
something wrong. But for a long time, I didn't know what it was.

     Finally, after listening carefully to many Japanese conversations, I
discovered what my problem was. Even though I was speaking
10   Japanese, I was handling the conversation[2] in a **Western** way.

     Japanese-style conversations develop quite differently from
Western-style conversations. And the difference isn't only in the
languages. I realized that just as I kept trying to hold Western-style
conversations even when I was speaking Japanese, so my English
15   students kept trying to hold Japanese-style conversations even when
they were speaking English. We were unconsciously playing entirely
different conversational ball games.

     A Western-style conversation between two people is like a game of
tennis. If I introduce a topic,[3] a conversational ball, I expect you to hit
20   it back. If you agree with me, I don't expect you simply to agree and do
nothing more. I expect you to add something - a reason for agreeing,
another example, or an elaboration[4] to carry the idea further. But I
don't expect you always to agree. I am just as happy if you question
me, or challenge me, or completely disagree with me. Whether you
25   agree or disagree, your response will return the ball to me.[5]

---

[1] **come to a halt**   stop

[2] **handling the conversation**   participating in the conversation

[3] **introduce a topic**   begin talking about something

[4] **elaboration**   detail

[5] **return the ball to me**   allow me to continue the conversation

And then it is my turn again. I don't serve a new ball from my original starting line. I hit your ball back again from where it has bounced.[6] I carry your idea further, or answer your questions or objections, or challenge or question you. And so the ball goes back and forth.

30

If there are more than two people in the conversation, then it is like doubles in tennis, or like **volleyball**. There's no waiting in line. Whoever is nearest and quickest hits the ball, and if you step back, someone else will hit it. No one stops the game to give you a turn.[7] You're responsible for taking your own turn.

35

But whether it's two players or a group, everyone does his or her best to keep the ball going, and no one person has the ball for very long.

A Japanese-style conversation, however, is not at all like tennis or volleyball. It's like **bowling**. You wait for your turn. And you always know your place in line. It depends on such things as whether you are older or younger, a close friend or a relative stranger[8] to the previous speaker, in a senior or junior position, and so on.

40

When your turn comes, you step up to the starting line with your bowling ball and carefully bowl it. Everyone else stands back and watches politely, murmuring encouragement.[9] Everyone waits until the ball has reached the end of the alley and watches to see if it knocks down all the pins, or only some of them, or none of them. There is a pause, while everyone registers[10] your score.

45

Then, after everyone is sure that you have completely finished your turn, the next person in line steps up to the same starting line, with a different ball. He doesn't return your ball, and he does not begin from where your ball stopped. And there is always a suitable pause between turns. There is no rush, no scramble[11] for the ball.

50

No wonder[12] everyone looked startled when I took part in Japanese conversations. I paid no attention to whose turn it was and

55

---

[6] **bounce**   hit the ground and go up again

[7] **give you a turn**   give you a chance to play

[8] **a relative stranger**   a comparative stranger; someone you don't know very well

[9] **murmuring encouragement**   giving encouragement in a soft voice

[10] **registers**   writes down on an official form

[11] **no scramble**   no competition; no fighting

[12] **No wonder**   It's not surprising

kept snatching the ball[13] halfway down the alley and throwing it back at the bowler. Of course the conversation died. I was playing the wrong game.

60   But if you have been trained all your life to play one game, it is no simple matter to switch to another, even if you know the rules. Knowing the rules is not at all the same thing as playing the game.

    Even now, during a conversation in Japanese, I will notice a startled reaction and belatedly realize[14] that once again I have rudely 65 interrupted by instinctively trying to hit back the other person's bowling ball. It is no easier for me to "just listen" during a conversation than it is for my Japanese students to "just relax" when speaking with foreigners. Now I can truly sympathize with how hard they must find it to try to carry on a Western-style conversation.[15]

About the Author

American **Nancy Sakamoto** wrote "Conversational Ball Games" while she was teaching English in Japan. She wrote about other experiences and cross-cultural observations of her life in Japan in a book called *Polite Fictions: Why Japanese and Americans Seem Rude to Each Other.*

---

[13] **snatching the ball**   quickly taking the ball from someone else; grabbing the ball

[14] **belatedly realize**   realize when it is too late

[15] **carry on a conversation**   have a conversation

After You Read

Understanding the Text

A. Multiple choice. For each item below, circle the answer that best completes the statement.

1. The main idea of this article is that _____.
   a. People converse differently in Japan than in the West.
   b. It's important to take part in conversations.
   c. It's difficult to have a conversation with someone from another country.
   d. It's rude to interrupt someone who is speaking.

2. The author makes all of the following arguments except _____.
   a. Japanese-style conversations are like bowling.
   b. Western-style conversations are like tennis or volleyball.
   c. In Japanese-style conversations, you must wait your turn to speak.
   d. Western-style conversations are longer than Japanese style conversations.

3. In line 47, the word *alley* probably means _____ in bowling.
   a. the place where you register your score
   b. the place where players sit
   c. something you wear
   d. the place where you roll the ball

4. You can infer from this article that the author _____.
   a. was born in Japan
   b. has always lived in Japan
   c. is a teacher
   d. no longer lives in Japan

5. The author's purpose in writing this article was *not* to _____.

   a. instruct

   b. entertain

   c. persuade

   d. criticize

6. The overall tone of the article is _____.

   a. serious and academic

   b. informative and personal

   c. humorous and unbelievable

   d. thoughtful and sad

B. Consider the issues. Work with a partner to answer the questions below.

   1. What are the characteristics of a Western-style conversation and a Japanese-style conversation? List ideas from the article in the chart below.

CONVERSATIONAL STYLES	
WESTERN	**JAPANESE**
okay to disagree	important to wait for your turn

   2. When you are having a conversation with a friend, is it more like a Western-style conversation or a Japanese-style conversation? Why?

   3. What is the author's attitude toward Western and Japanese-style conversations? Does she think one style is better than the other?

Identifying Organizational Patterns

As you read, it's helpful to understand how the ideas in a piece of writing are organized. Below are three commonly-used **organizational patterns** in English.

Organized by time. When writers tell a story, they often present the events in the story in the order in which they happened. Dates and time phrases (*at 4 p.m.; then; when I was 16*) indicate that the writing is organized by time.

Organized by order of importance. When writers want to explain something, they may provide their reasons or examples starting with the most important information and ending with the least important. Alternatively, they may start with the least important information and end with the most important.

Organized by differences. When writers want to show how two things are different, they can first describe one thing in detail and then go on to describe the other thing. Alternatively, they can contrast the differences between the two things.

Look back at the readings below and identify the general organizational pattern. Write **Time**, **Order of Importance**, or **Differences**. Share your ideas with a partner.

TITLE OF READING	ORGANIZATIONAL PATTERN
1. Conversational Ball Games (page 158)	_____
2. A Long Walk Home (page 4)	_____
3. Student Learning Teams (page 14)	_____
4. Culture Shock (page 26)	_____
5. Private Lives (page 72)	_____

> ### Prefixes
> You can add a **prefix** to certain words to add the meaning *not* to the word. For example, the word *unconscious* means *not conscious.*
>
> **Prefixes that mean not:**
> > un-   in-   ir-   ab-   dis-   im-

A. Add a prefix from the box to each word below to add the meaning "not" to the word. The first one is done for you.

1. a *suitable* pause   _an unsuitable pause_

2. a *responsible* person   _____

3. an *original* idea   _____

4. an *agreeable* person   _____

5. an *appropriate* response   _____

6. a *proper* remark   _____

7. an *effective* strategy   _____

8. an *adventurous* student   _____

9. a *formal* relationship   _____

10. a *normal* request   _____

11. a *democratic* society   _____

12. a *conventional* idea   _____

B. Look in a dictionary to find more examples of adjectives with a prefix meaning **not** and write them in the chart below.

UN_____	IN_____	IR_____
unpopular	incomplete	irreversible

Conditional statements

A **factual conditional** tells what happens usually or in general. We often use the factual conditional when we are talking about rules or habits:

In tennis, if you hit the ball out of the court, your partner gets a point. Whether it's two players or a group, everyone does his or her best to keep the ball going.

A **future conditional** tells what might happen in the future:

If you miss the next ball, we'll lose the game.
I'll play whether or not you do.

A. The paragraphs below are from the article on pages 158–160. Read each paragraph and underline the conditional statements. In the margin, write **factual conditional** or **future conditional**.

factual
conditional

1. A Western-style conversation between two people is like a game of tennis. <u>If I introduce a topic, a conversational ball, I expect you to hit it back.</u> If you agree with me, I don't expect you simply to agree and do nothing more. I expect you to add something - a reason for agreeing, another example, or an elaboration to carry the idea further. But I don't expect you always to agree. I am just as happy if you question me, or challenge me, or completely disagree with me. Whether you agree or disagree, your response will return the ball to me.

2. If there are more than two people in the conversation, then it is like doubles in tennis, or like volleyball. There's no waiting in line. Whoever is nearest and quickest hits the ball, and if you step back, someone else will hit it. No one stops the game to give you a turn. You're responsible for taking your own turn.

B. Use the factual conditional to complete these statements with your own ideas.

a. If someone interrupts me, I usually _____

_____

b. If I disagree with someone, I usually _____

_____

c. If I can't get to sleep, I usually _____

_____

Discussion & Writing

A. Is the conversation below a Japanese-style conversation or a Western-style conversation? Why do you think so?

Paul: What did you think of the movie?
Susan: I thought it was great — especially the ending.
Paul: Really? Didn't you think it was sad?
Susan: Well, a little bit, but it was funny, too.
Paul: What do you mean?
Susan: . . .

B. According to the author, what could you say to keep this conversation going Western-style? Write three possible responses to John's statement in the boxes below.

John: Australia is the best place to go on vacation.

1. Agree and then add something.	**2.** Ask a question.	**3.** Disagree and add something.
_____ _____ _____	_____ _____ _____	_____ _____ _____

C. Complete the opinions below. Then read one of your opinions to a partner and see how long you can keep a Western-style conversation going.

1. I think _____ is a really good movie.

2. _____ is a great place for a vacation.

3. I think it's dangerous to _____

4. _____ [your own idea]

Crossword Puzzle

Use words from the reading to complete the crossword puzzle.

Across:

1 The opposite of *sad* is ___.

3 Another word for *stop* is ___. (line 5)

4 Another way to say *have a conversation* is ___ a conversation. (line 13)

7 In tennis, two people play a singles match while four people play a ___ match. (line 32)

9 Tennis players try to hit the ball back and ___ over the net. (line 30)

10 The opposite of *encourage* is ___.

13 ___, subtract, multiply, divide

14 In bowling, you try to knock over all of the ___.

15 The past form of *have* is ___.

17 Another word for *completely* is ___. (line 16)

Down:

1 In tennis, you don't throw the ball; you ___ it.

2 The past tense of *pay* is ___.

5 The opposite of *the same* is ___.

6 A word for *slowly* or *a little at a time* is ___. (line 2)

8 Another word for *surprised* is ___. (line 55)

10 The opposite of *agree* is ___.

11 The opposite of *complicated* is ___.

12 am, ___, are

16 An opposite of *none* is ___.

Spain (map on page 190)   Spain is the third largest country in
Europe, and is located in the southwestern corner of the continent.
The population of Spain is 39,000,000 and tourism brings 57,000,000
visitors each year. Madrid, located in the middle of the country, is the
capital. Other important cities include Barcelona, Valencia, Seville,
and Granada.

miles   One mile is equal to 1.61 kilometers. The United States is one of
the only countries in the world that still uses the English system for
weights and measurements. The following chart show some of the
different measurements in the English and metric systems:

ENGLISH SYSTEM	METRIC SYSTEM
1 inch	2.54 centimeters
1 foot	0.305 meters
1 yard	0.914 meters
1 mile	1.61 kilometers

Chapter 2 – Culture and Language Notes

Harvard University   Harvard University is the oldest and most famous university in North America. Founded in 1636, Harvard is a private university located in Cambridge, Massachusetts, near Boston. There are about 18,000 undergraduate and graduate students at Harvard and 2,000 faculty members. John F. Kennedy and five other United States presidents were Harvard University graduates, and more than thirty members of its faculty have been Nobel Prize winners.

senior   Seniors are students in their final year of high school or college. First-year students are called *freshmen*, second-year students are *sophomores*, and students in their third year of high school or college are *juniors*.

study group   See *learning team* below.

learning team   A learning team, also called a *study group*, is a group of students that meets on a regular basis to talk about class readings, study for exams, and do other things to improve the students' grades. Research has shown that students who study together outside of class often do better than students who only study on their own.

highlighting and margin notes   Highlighting and taking margin notes are two ways to help you record and remember important information when you read. You highlight by using a colored pen to mark the important words, sentences, or paragraphs that you want to remember and review later. You write margin notes next to important ideas in the book you are reading. (The margin is the white space on the page.) Your margin notes could be of various types:

- General reactions to the reading (e.g., *Great idea!*)
- Connections between the reading and your own life (e.g., *This city sounds like the place where I grew up.*)
- Questions about the reading (e.g., *What is the main idea here?*)

Writing margin notes helps you read more actively and effectively.

office hours   Most professors in American universities hold office hours every week to help students with any questions they have. Professors usually set aside three to four hours at the same time each week for their office hours. Students usually do not need to make an appointment to visit their professors during office hours; they can simply stop by.

national survey   A national survey is used to find out public opinion on a particular issue. There are professional groups and companies that take national surveys. They ask hundreds or thousands of people the same set of questions and then report the results. Many businesses use national surveys to see how popular or effective their products are. During election campaigns, national surveys are often used to show how popular the different candidates are, or how the voters feel about specific political issues.

culture shock   "Culture shock" is the feeling some people experience when they travel to a new country or part of the world for the first time. Sometimes the food, style of dress, and other aspects of life in a new country are so different that people have a hard time adjusting to this new way of life. Culture shock can last for days, weeks, or even months.

Melbourne (map on page 191)   Melbourne is the capital of Victoria, a state in the southeastern part of Australia. There are roughly 3,300,000 people in Melbourne, the second largest city in Australia after Sydney. Melbourne was established by English settlers in 1835, and is the youngest city of its size in the world. It is a busy trade and manufacturing center that has attracted immigrants from many countries, including Greece, Italy, Poland, Turkey, China, Cambodia, and Vietnam.

Boston College   Boston College (BC) is a major university located just outside Boston in Chestnut Hill, Massachusetts. Founded in 1863, BC is one of the oldest and largest Catholic universities in the United States, with 8,700 undergraduates and 4,500 graduate students. In 1999, there were students from 85 different countries at BC.

exchange students   Exchange students go to schools or universities outside of their home countries. Each year, more than 1,200,000 students around the world leave their home countries to study abroad. Roughly 470,000 international students each year come to study in the United States, while about 70,000 Americans study abroad each year. Many American colleges and universities recruit foreign students to study in their undergraduate and graduate programs. Foreign students bring an international perspective to campuses, teaching Americans about other countries and cultures.

Boston (map on page 192)   Boston is the capital of the state of Massachusetts, about 200 miles north of New York City on the Atlantic Ocean. About 550,000 people live in the city itself, and about 2,500,000 live in the surrounding suburbs. Boston is one of the oldest and most historically important cities in North America, and was founded in 1630. The Revolutionary War between the American colonies and England began near Boston in 1775. Boston is known for its fine universities, beautiful architecture, and delicious seafood.

Australia (map on page 191)   Australia is the smallest continent on the planet and also one of the largest countries. It is located south of Asia between the Indian and Pacific Oceans. Australia's capital is Canberra, and the largest cities are Sydney, Melbourne, Brisbane, and Perth. The population of Australia is roughly 18,000,000 people, with 85% living in cities. The koala bear, kangaroo, and several other Australian animals are not found anywhere else in the world.

Massachusetts (map on page 192)   Massachusetts is a state located on the Atlantic Ocean northeast of New York City. It was one of the thirteen original American colonies. These colonies got their independence from England in 1783 when they became the United States of America. Today, more than 6,000,000 people live in Massachusetts. Roughly half the population lives in and around the capital city of Boston.

eating disorders   An eating disorder is a medical condition caused by the intense fear of being overweight. A person with an eating disorder uses dangerous methods to stay thin, including starvation or abuse of diet pills. This behavior can result in serious health problems. Some researchers believe that 20 percent of all American women in high school and college have shown symptoms of an eating disorder at some time.

legal drinking age of 21   In the United States, the legal drinking age is 21, which means you must be 21 years old to buy alcoholic drinks. The legal drinking age is 21 in some other countries, including Korea, Malaysia, and the Ukraine. In Brazil, Hong Kong, the United Kingdom, and most other countries around the world, however, the drinking age is 18. The legal drinking age in Canada is 19, and in Japan it is 20. In France, Spain, and several other European countries, people may drink alcohol when they are 16.

sophomore   Sophomores are students in their second year of high school or college. First-year students are called *freshmen*, third-year students are called *juniors*, and students in their fourth year of high school or college are called *seniors*.

work part-time   Many North American high school and university students work part-time while attending school. These students typically work 5 to 15 hours each week in the afternoons and evenings, or on the weekends. A lot of students find part-time work in restaurants and retail stores, or as baby-sitters. In general, people must be 16 years old to work legally in the United States.

straight As   American students who get straight As usually score between 90 and 100 percent on all of their tests and receive a grade of A in all of their courses. The following chart shows the different grades given to students in the United States and the corresponding percentages.

GRADE	PERCENTAGE (%)
A	90–100
B	80–89
C	70–79
D	60–69
F (Fail)	0–59
P (Pass)	60–100

Some schools or universities add a plus sign (+) or a minus sign (–) after the letter grades to give more specific information about a student's performance.

Braille   Braille is a system of writing for the blind in which patterns of raised dots represent letters, letter combinations (such as *ch*), some commonly used short words, numbers, and punctuation marks. It can also be used for writing music. Blind people read Braille by running their fingers over rows of the dot patterns. They can write in Braille by making the dot patterns themselves, using special equipment.

traditional music   Most countries have traditional forms of music that represent their culture and customs. Traditional music is sometimes called *folk music*.

jazz   Jazz is a truly American form of music. It was developed in the early 1900s and has its roots in African American music. Dixieland jazz and the trumpet player Louis Armstrong came out of New Orleans, Louisiana, and became a sensation in the 1920s. In the 1930s jazz achieved a peak of popularity. During this period, known as the "Swing Era," Americans were dancing to "swing" music inspired by the bands of Duke Ellington and Fletcher Henderson. Since that time, jazz has taken various forms, including bebop, modal jazz, and fusion jazz to name a few. Jazz continues to be a popular form of music both in the United States and around the world.

Lee Fong Gwo   The singer's aboriginal name is *Difang Duana*, but he is widely recognized by his Mandarin name, *Kuo Ying-Nan*. The name *Lee Fong Gwo* used in this transcript is non-standard and probably written at a time when the different names and their spellings were not commonly understood outside of Taiwan.

pop charts   All over the world, the most popular current songs are listed each week on pop charts. Radio stations play pop music, and the songs these stations play are selected from each week's pop chart.

town council   Many American cities and towns elect a local government, called a town council or city council. Many town council meetings are open to the public, and it is common for Americans to attend these meetings and express their opinions on local issues such as taxes and schools.

property taxes   Nearly all American homeowners and landowners pay property taxes each year on the value of their home and/or land. Property taxes are obligatory payments to the government, and this money is used for education, building roads, and the costs of other vital services.

political rally   A large meeting held to support a politician or someone running for public office is called a political rally. At political rallies, you often hear loud music and shouting, as these events are designed to excite people about a politician's ideas.

Mark Twain (1835 –1910)   Mark Twain, one of America's most famous authors, is best known for his novels *The Adventures of Tom Sawyer* and *The Adventures of Huckleberry Finn,* which are stories of life along the Mississippi River. These novels have become classics of American literature. Mark Twain was also a very talented public speaker who went on a lecture tour of the world in 1894.

tribute to the company treasurer on his retirement   When an American businessperson leaves his or her job after many years of work, the company usually throws a retirement party. At the party, colleagues typically pay tribute to the person by giving toasts, making short speeches, and telling stories about that person's contributions to the company.

Edward R. Murrow (1908–1965)   Edward R. Murrow was one of the greatest American radio and television journalists. He was a brave reporter who provided Americans with radio news throughout World War II. Murrow became famous for his broadcasts from London's rooftops during the German bombing of that city. After World War II, Murrow returned to the United States and produced several popular television news programs. He was known throughout his life as an excellent public speaker.

Gulf of Mexico (map on page 192)   The Gulf of Mexico is bordered by Mexico to the west and south, Texas and other U.S. states to the north, and the coast of Florida to the east. The ocean water in the Gulf of Mexico is calm and warm.

Super 8 movie   Super 8mm film was a popular technology for making home movies in the 1960s and 1970s. These were called Super 8 movies. Parents would make movies of their families on vacation, during holidays, and on other special occasions. Videotape technology replaced Super 8 cameras in the 1980s, as video was easier and cheaper to use.

North Carolina (map on page 192)   North Carolina is an American state located in the southeastern part of the country along the Atlantic Ocean. North Carolina borders the states of Virginia, South Carolina, Tennessee, and Georgia. More than 7,000,000 people live in North Carolina, the tenth largest state by population in the United States. Raleigh is the capital, and Charlotte is its largest city.

Florida (map on page 192)   Florida, America's number one tourist destination, is called The Sunshine State, and is located in the southeastern corner of the United States. The weather is sunny and warm most of the year there. There are miles and miles of beaches in Florida along the Atlantic Ocean and the Gulf of Mexico. Tallahassee, situated in the northern part of the state, is the capital, and Miami is the largest city.

boyfriend   In North America, *boyfriend* means a man of any age who has a romantic relationship with someone else. *Girlfriend* is a similar expression that means a woman of any age who has a romantic relationship with someone else. However, a woman may also use the word *girlfriend* to refer to a woman friend.

Bill Gates (1955 –) William H. (Bill) Gates, one of the richest people on earth, is the founder of Microsoft Corporation, the largest developer of computer software in the world. He wrote his first computer program at age 13, went to Harvard University for two years, and then dropped out at age 20 to start Microsoft with his friend, Paul Allen. In 1981, Microsoft produced its first successful product, a computer operating system called MS-DOS. In the next few years, the company released Microsoft Word and Windows, very successful software programs that sold millions of copies in the 1980s and 1990s. In 1995, Gates made a big decision to begin developing products for the Internet. He has donated billions of dollars for health care and for improving student access to computers and other new technologies.

stock ticker A stock ticker is an electronic sign that gives people information about the current value of a share of stock in each company. Letters and numbers move quickly across a stock ticker. This information helps investors know if the stocks they own are increasing or decreasing in value.

videoconferencing Videoconferencing is a technology that allows people in different places to see and talk to each other. During a videoconference, you can look at a television screen and communicate with other people sitting in a room far away. Videoconferencing technology uses telephone lines to deliver pictures and sounds from one location to another.

letter of application   If you are interested in working for an American company, you usually send a letter of application and a resume to the company's personnel or human resources department. Note that a letter of application is often called a *cover letter*.

résumé   A résumé is a short summary of your education and job history that you send to a company when you are looking for a job. Most résumés are one to three pages long and include only the highlights of your educational and professional experience. In the United States, you should always include a letter of application or cover letter with your résumé when you are applying for a job.

help-wanted ad   Many people in the United States find their jobs through help-wanted ads in newspapers. Generally, the Sunday newspaper in most cities carries a large number of help-wanted ads. When people are looking for a job, they review the ads and then send a letter of application and résumé to the companies where they would like to work. In the past few years, most companies have begun to advertise their job openings on websites as well.

personnel   The personnel department, also called the human resources department, handles the interviewing, hiring, and training of new employees in a company. It is also responsible for handling benefits like health insurance and retirement plans. If a company decides that an employee should be fired, the personnel department handles this process as well.

district attorney   A district attorney is a lawyer in the United States who works for the government. Many Americans refer to a district attorney as a D.A. A district attorney is usually responsible for prosecuting crimes within a particular area.

reference   A reference can be two things. A reference can be a *letter* giving information about your skills and personality. This letter is usually written by a former teacher or employer and is often sent to a company for which you would like to work. A reference can also be a *person* whom an employer contacts to ask questions about your background.

executive assistant An executive assistant works for an executive in a company, assisting in all aspects of office work. Executive assistants have excellent organizational, computer, and communication skills, and are often paid very well.

Spain   See *Spain* on page 168.

Common Market (map on page 190)   The official name for the Common Market is the European Union (EU). The fifteen countries in the EU cooperate in a variety of economic and political areas. In 1999, the EU introduced the euro, a new currency that can be used in many European countries. In 2002, the euro replaced local currencies such as the German mark and French franc, and became the official currency in 12 member countries.

EU countries are: Austria, Belgium, Denmark, Finland, France, Germany, Greece, Ireland, Italy, Luxembourg, the Netherlands, Portugal, Spain, Sweden, and the United Kingdom.

siesta   *Siesta* is the Spanish word for a nap or a short period of sleep in the middle of the day. Many people in Spain and Latin America take a siesta in the afternoon following their lunch. The typical siesta is from 2:00 to 4:30. In the past, almost everyone in Spain took a siesta every day. While this tradition is still popular, fewer people stop for a siesta nowadays. Especially in large cities like Madrid and Barcelona, many professional people work from 9:00 to 5:00 with only a short break for lunch. Some people think Spain is losing part of its rich culture when companies don't allow their employees to enjoy a long lunch and siesta in the middle of the day. Other people, however, think that this kind of change is necessary for Spain's economic growth.

Madrid (map on page 190)   Madrid, a city of 3,000,000 people, is the capital of Spain. Located at roughly 2,000 feet (600 meters) above sea level, Madrid is a city with very hot summers and cool winters. The Palacio Real, the enormous royal palace where Spain's king and queen live, is located in the middle of the city.

standard of living   The *standard of living* is a way to describe the quality of living conditions for an individual or of a country. You can measure the standard of living in a country by looking at the average salary, the general quality of housing and health care, the availability of good food, educational opportunities, etc. The adjectives *high* and *low* describe the standard of living in a country or region; *The standard of living in Sweden is high.*

Frankenstein   The creature from the Frankenstein movies is the best-known monster in movie history. Originally, Frankenstein was the character in a novel by Mary Shelley. This novel, and many of the films based on it, is the story of a "mad scientist" who creates a monster that eventually kills him. The famous Hollywood movie *Frankenstein* (1931) is based on Shelley's novel.

science fiction   Science fiction is a kind of fiction that deals with possible future results of new technologies. Science fiction books and movies often deal with people living in space or with aliens from other worlds who visit Earth. Famous science fiction writers include Isaac Asimov and Ray Bradbury. The *Star Wars* and *Star Trek* films are some of the most popular and famous science fiction movies of the late 20th century.

acid rain   Acid rain contains a level of acid that is harmful to the environment. It is normal for rainwater to have a certain amount of acid. However, when dangerous chemicals from cars and factories mix with rain, the percentage of acid in the rain can become too high. When this acid rain falls, it can hurt or kill plants and animals.

greenhouse effect   *The greenhouse effect* refers to the way that gases in the atmosphere around the Earth act like the glass ceiling in a greenhouse. Greenhouses are glass buildings that cover flowers and plants so that they can stay warm and grow even in the winter. Like a greenhouse, the Earth's atmosphere keeps the heat from the Sun near the Earth so that we stay warm. In recent years, scientists have found that some forms of air pollution in the atmosphere are keeping more heat inside. If greenhouse gases continue to increase, rising temperatures could cause climate changes and result in environmental disasters.

genetic engineering   Genetic engineering is a very new area of science that deals with studying and changing the natural development of plants and animals. By changing the DNA or genetic structure of a living thing, scientists can affect the way it grows. For example, they can create new kinds of tomatoes that stay fresh longer. Many people think that this example demonstrates a good use of genetic engineering. However, others feel that modifying living things in this way may not be completely safe in the long term. And most people think that scientists should never use genetic engineering to clone people; that is, to make an exact copy of a human being.

East-West tensions   After World War II, the communist Soviet Union had control of eastern Europe, while the governments of western Europe and other democracies like the United States and Canada cooperated with each other to fight the spread of communism. This period of East-West tensions was called the Cold War. During the Cold War, countries on both sides built nuclear weapons and developed strong armies in case they had to go to war. In the late 1980s, however, many countries in eastern Europe began to reject Soviet control and demand freedom. By 1995, there were democracies throughout eastern Europe and the former Soviet Union. During the 1990s, East-West tensions were greatly reduced.

graduate student   A graduate student is a person who has received his or her bachelor's degree and who is studying to receive a master's or doctorate. The chart below provides information on the most popular types of graduate programs in North America:

Graduate School	Degree	Number of Years of Study	Career Goal
Medical	M.D. (doctor of medicine)	4	doctor
Law	J.D. (juris doctor)	3	lawyer
Business	M.B.A. (master of business administration)	2	business executive
Arts and Science	M.A. (master of art), M.S. (master of science), or Ph.D. (doctor of philosophy)	Master's 2 Doctorate 4–6	Professor and various other professions

dowry   A dowry is the money or valuables that a bride receives from her parents at the time of her marriage. In some cultures, a dowry is supposed to give a woman some financial support in the event her husband dies. The custom of dowries is still widely practiced in some places.

cash gift   In North America, as in many other parts of the world, cash gifts are often given as presents. Typically, older people give cash gifts to younger people to celebrate birthdays, graduations, or holidays like Christmas. In America, it is unusual for people to give cash gifts to their friends or to older relatives. When giving a cash gift, people often put cash or a check inside a greeting card.

toast   When you drink in someone's honor, you *toast* them. To propose a toast in the United States, everyone is served a drink and one person makes a short speech. A traditional toast at a wedding might be: *Please join me in wishing the newlyweds health and happiness. To (bride's name) and (groom's name).* Then, everyone raises their glasses and takes a drink together.

Chapter 13 — Culture and Language Notes

Mona Lisa   The *Mona Lisa* is probably the most famous painting in Western art. It was painted by Leonardo da Vinci in 1504. Thousands of people see the *Mona Lisa* every day in the Louvre Museum in Paris. The *Mona Lisa* is a small picture of a wealthy woman from Florence, Italy, who seems to be smiling very slightly. For 500 years, people have talked about what this mysterious smile means.

theory of relativity   Albert Einstein (1879 –1955) is one of the greatest scientists the world has ever known. His general theory of relativity explains his theory of gravity, as well as more general scientific concepts. (*Gravity* refers to the force which causes objects to fall toward Earth.) Published in 1915, Einstein's theory of relativity is a general framework that allows us to understand the birth of our universe, its current structure, and ideas about the future development of the solar system.

Galileo Galilei (1564 –1642)   Galileo was a famous Italian astronomer and mathematician. After developing the first telescope, Galileo spent much of his time observing and writing about the stars and planets. He was the first to discover, for example, the moons around the planet Jupiter.

Thomas Alva Edison (1847–1931)   The American inventor Thomas Alva Edison is responsible for a large number of inventions that have changed our world. He is best known for inventing the light bulb and the record player, but these are only two of his more than 1000 inventions. Edison also developed the carbon transmitter that allowed Alexander Graham Bell to invent the telephone.

Wolfgang Amadeus Mozart   (1756 –1791)   The Austrian musician Wolfgang Amadeus Mozart was one of the greatest composers of classical music. Mozart was an amazing child who could play and write great music by the age of six. During his short life, Mozart composed more than 600 pieces of music. These include the operas *The Marriage of Figaro* and *Don Giovanni* as well as 41 symphonies and many concertos. *Amadeus* is a popular American film about the composer's life.

René Descartes (1596 –1650)   René Descartes is often called the father of modern philosophy. He developed a way of thinking called rationalism. Descartes' most famous quotation is: *I think, therefore I am*. The meaning of this quote is discussed in philosophy courses all over the world.

Charles Dickens (1812–1870)   Charles Dickens was one of the most brilliant English novelists in history. Born in Hampshire, England, Dickens became a journalist as a young man, and then started writing novels. His most famous books include *Oliver Twist, David Copperfield, A Tale of Two Cities*, and *Great Expectations*. Most of Dickens' books described important social problems that are still relevant today.

Charles Darwin (1809 –1882)   Charles Darwin was an English scientist who is best known for his theory of evolution. In one of Darwin's last books, *The Descent of Man*, he argued that human beings had evolved from apes. These ideas were extremely controversial in the late 19th century, and are still debated today.

IQ   An IQ is used to measure a person's level of intelligence. The letters *IQ* stand for *intelligence quotient*. IQ tests measure certain mental abilities that have been traditionally associated with intelligence. On an IQ test, the average score is 100. Many people argue that an IQ test is not a good way to measure a person's intelligence, because it only tests a few abilities. In the past few years, many people have argued that we should look at many factors when measuring a person's intelligence, such as the ability to get along with others, athletic skills, or musical ability.

Nobel Prize   Six Nobel Prizes are given each year to people who have made the most important contributions in the fields of physics, chemistry, medicine, economics, and literature, as well as the person or people who have done the most to promote peace in the world. The Nobel Prizes were established by the Swedish inventor Alfred Bernhard Nobel, and were first given in 1901. Receiving a Nobel Prize is considered by many to be one of the greatest honors in the world.

Richard Feynman (1918 –1988)   Richard Feynman was an American physicist from New York who is most famous for his work on the Manhattan Project from 1941 to 1945. On this top-secret project, Feynman and a group of other scientists worked to develop the first atomic bombs. Twenty years later, Feynman won the 1965 Nobel Prize in physics for his work in a field called *quantum electrodynamics*.

Sigmund Freud (1856 –1939) Sigmund Freud is the father of psychoanalysis and the most important person in the history of psychology. Psychoanalysis is a medical method of curing mental illness. Freud was an Austrian doctor who began experimenting in the 1890s with a "talking cure" to assist his patients who were mentally ill. In 1900, Freud published his most important book, *The Interpretation of Dreams*. Throughout his career, Freud argued that thinking and talking about your dreams was an important way to achieve mental health.

Roman numerals Roman numerals were used 2000 years ago during the time of the Roman Empire and are still used today. The chart below compares Roman numerals with the more common Arabic numerals.

ROMAN NUMERALS	ARABIC NUMERALS
I	1
V	5
X	10
L	50
C	100
D	500
M	1000

Here are some examples of Roman numerals and their values:

VI = 6 (5 + 1)
CM = 900 (1000 - 100)
CX = 110 (100 + 10)

Today, Roman numerals are often seen on the outside of important buildings. These numbers show the year in which a building was built. For example, MCMLX = 1960.

Renaissance *Renaissance* is a French word that means *rebirth*. We use this term to refer to the period in Europe between roughly 1400 and 1550. For more than 1000 years, the writings and the art of the Greeks and Romans had been forgotten by Europeans. The Renaissance was a time of "rebirth" because of the new interest in classical Greek and Roman art and ideas. Great masterpieces like da Vinci's *Mona Lisa* and Michelangelo's statue *David* were completed during the *High Renaissance*, the final years of this period in history.

Leonardo da Vinci (1452 –1519)   Leonardo da Vinci was a remarkable man; an exceptional painter, architect, sculptor, and engineer, he was perhaps the greatest genius of the Italian Renaissance. His most famous painting is the *Mona Lisa*. Da Vinci's notebooks show his amazing understanding of the human body, as well as his creative ideas for many inventions that we have today, including the contact lens and the airplane.

Johann Sebastian Bach (1685 –1750)   Johann Sebastian Bach was one of Europe's greatest composers of classical music. Bach was born into a musical German family, and learned to play the organ at an early age. He began composing music as a young man. Bach's most famous musical works include the *Brandenburg Concertos* and the *Mass in B Minor*.

Gregor Mendel (1822 –1884)   Gregor Mendel was an Austrian scientist who spent much of his life researching the ways plants and animals change over many generations. He is known today as the father of modern genetics. Genetics is the study of how physical characteristics are passed from parents to children, and Mendel dedicated his life to understanding and writing about this process.

Japan   Located in northeast Asia, Japan is comprised of roughly 3900 islands with 16,800 miles (27,000 kilometers) of coastline. The four largest Japanese islands are Kyushu, Shikoku, Hokkaido, and Honshu. The Pacific Ocean lies to the east of Japan, and the Sea of Japan is on the west side. With a population of 125.9 million, Japan is one of the most densely populated countries in the world. Roughly 30 million people live in and around Tokyo, the nation's capital.

Western   The term *Western* refers to people, places, or things relating to *the West*, the group of countries including Europe and America that share a heritage from Ancient Greece and the Roman Empire. We can, for example, refer to cars manufactured in Sweden, Germany, or the United States as Western cars. A person from the West is sometimes called a *Westerner*.

We use the term *Eastern* to talk about Asian people, places, or things. We refer to Buddhism, for example, as an Eastern religion. When people refer to the *Far East*, they are talking about Japan, China, Korea, and other countries in this easternmost region of Asia.

tennis   An early version of the game of tennis was played in French monasteries as early as the 11th century. The monks used their hands to hit the ball back and forth over a piece of rope. Tennis racquets with strings were invented by 1500. Originally an indoor sport, an outdoor version of tennis played on grass was invented in 1858. Tennis came to the United States in 1874 and was on the program for the first modern Olympic Games in 1896. Played both indoors and outdoors, tennis is enjoyed by more than 43 million people around the world.

volleyball   Volleyball was invented in the United States just over 100 years ago when William G. Morgan decided to blend the elements of basketball, baseball, tennis, and handball to create an exciting game that would involve minimal physical contact. Volleyball is tremendously popular around the world. Indoor volleyball became an Olympic sport in 1964 during the Tokyo Olympics, while beach volleyball was introduced at Atlanta's Summer Olympic Games in 1996. First made popular on the beaches of California, beach volleyball is now played throughout the world and is especially popular with Brazilians and others living in warm climates.

bowling Enjoyed in over 90 countries around the world, bowling is especially popular in the United States where 80 million people bowl at least once in a while.

A discovery of objects found in an Egyptian grave seems to suggest that the sport has been around since 3200 B.C. Some historians suggest that bowling really started in Germany around AD 300 and spread to Holland and later England. These Europeans took the sport to the United States where it became firmly established in the late 1900s. Bowling enjoyed a burst of popularity in the 1950s when TV bowling shows like *Celebrity Bowling* and *Bowling for Dollars* were hits.

Map 1 **Europe**

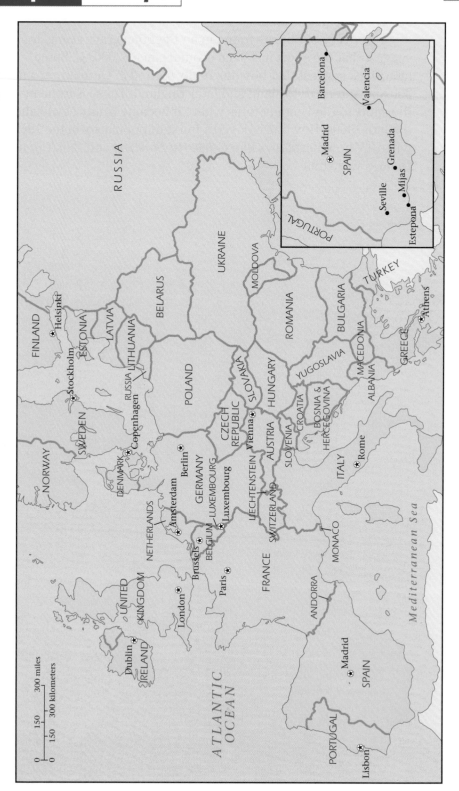

Map 2 | **Australia**

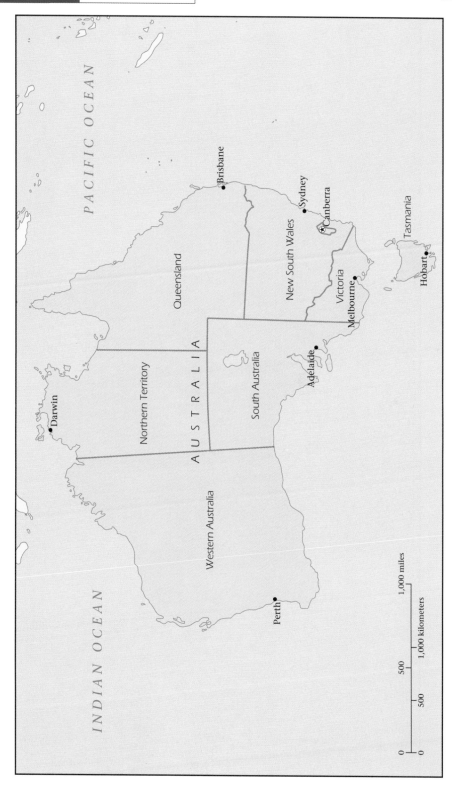

Map 3 Eastern United States

CANADA

Cambridge • • Boston

Massachusetts

North Carolina

Mississippi

Alabama

ATLANTIC
OCEAN

Texas

Louisiana

★Tallahassee

Florida

Gulf of Mexico

| 0 | 125 | 250 miles |
| 0 | 125 | 250 kilometers |

Map 4   **Japan and Taiwan**

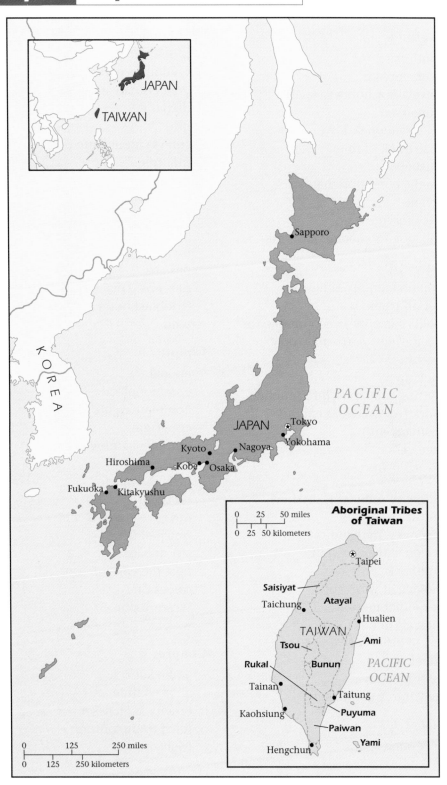

JAPAN

TAIWAN

● Sapporo

K O R E A

*PACIFIC
OCEAN*

JAPAN

⍟ Tokyo

Kyoto ●   ● Nagoya   ● Yokohama

Hiroshima ●   Kobe ●   ● Osaka

Fukuoka ●   ● Kitakyushu

0   125   250 miles
0   125   250 kilometers

**Aboriginal Tribes
of Taiwan**

0   25   50 miles
0   25   50 kilometers

⍟ Taipei

Saisiyat

Taichung ●

Atayal

● Hualien

TAIWAN

Tsou

Ami

Rukal

Bunun

Tainan ●

● Taitung

Kaohsiung ●

Puyuma

*PACIFIC
OCEAN*

Paiwan

Yami

Hengchun ●

Vocabulary Index

Chapter 1

confess to
contemplate
have a few hours to spare
immersed
let (someone) down
lose track of time
misbehave
on the condition that
relent
(be) serviced
the look (someone) gave me

Chapter 2

complementary skills
get off track
hold (someone) accountable for
mastering a particular topic
peers
pick up
putting principles into practice
shirk (one's) responsibility
team up with
vice versa

Chapter 3

adjust to American rhythms
culture trauma
discover firsthand
get on with (one's) life
laid-back
moving at warp speed
perpetual-motion machines
pick at (one's) food
sea of difference
shocker
taste a lifestyle
tuck into a good meal

Chapter 4

accessing

at home with
block out
computer networks
conceptualize
disparate
grid
(one's) immediate boss
innards
locate
logbook
merger
on call
owing more to
pass to
perceived disability
troubleshooter
whiz

Chapter 5

appeal
commonplace
complete rights
copyright
ethnomusicologist
fade into
he is the music
hit record
never received a cent
rice paddies
stir debate
take the case of
traces of
Western pop
wok

Chapter 6

ad-lib speech
allotted time
brevity is an asset
filled to the rafters
fright-frozen

good-natured story
intents
keyed up
lighthearted in tone
peek out
round out (one's) material
the so-called "butterflies"
the uninitiated

Chapter 7

burgundy hair
feed off the sea
fragile
glistening
hang out
play over and over
sanctuary
sheer force
talk (someone) into

Chapter 8

access information
cable television
corporate intranets
drug-infested
fail to grasp
full complement of
(be) penalized at grade time
penmanship
recipient
resemble
shut down
(be) the exception rather than
    the rule
the notion of
when the power goes out

Chapter 9

broach the subject
check where things stand
(be) composed with distinction
grant (someone) an interview
hit the mark
mass of other qualified applicants
most pertinent characteristics

mundane opening
negotiable
pat (oneself) on the back
redundant
résumé
sell (one's) qualifications
the job at hand
verifiable facts
(be) written with flair

Chapter 10

a few z's
a thousand degrees
attend to
biological clocks
biorhythm
blast furnaces
civil servants
from pole to pole
ghost town
incineration
key component
live on
new circadian order
nocturnal orbit
nod out
offices empty
out on the town
social imperative
stroll
technocrat
wink off
work operates under the
    command of life

Chapter 11

alien civilization
ambivalent attitude
    toward science
basic framework
harness an interest
inquiring minds
learn by rote
Northern Hemisphere
our stage

(be) poised to strike
privileged minority
qualitative grasp of
recede from public
 consciousness
sick joke
transistors
trigger

Chapter 12

cajole (someone) to
conventional
distinguished
easygoing
evenly
extravagant
fluster
give you big face
in tow
infuriate
lose (one's) cool
marital intentions
Messrs.
muddled
prospective
suffer a loss of face
swallow hard
third party
touchy

Chapter 13

become fixated on (one's)
 pre-conceived plan
building blocks
cantata
celibate
contemporaries

conventional response
facility
foster rigidity
halve 13
heredity
highest order
hold patents
idea quota
illuminate
lead (someone) astray
look at (something) from all
 angles
mark of genius
paradigm
reconceptualize the problem
run-of-the-mill
spawn
unveil

Chapter 14

belatedly realize
bounce
carry on a conversation
come to a halt
elaboration
give (someone) a turn
handling the conversation
introduce a topic
murmuring encouragement
no scramble
no wonder
register
relative stranger
return the ball to (someone)
snatching the ball